Activating the Power Within

8 WEEKS TO AN EMPOWERED LIFE

WAUKENA ANN CUYJET

BALBOA.
PRESS

A DIVISION OF HAY HOUSE

ISBN: 978-1-4525-4298-0 (sc)
ISBN: 978-1-4525-4297-3 (e)

Library of Congress Control Number: 2011961412

Balboa Press books may be ordered through booksellers or by contacting:

Balboa Press
A Division of Hay House
1663 Liberty Drive
Bloomington, IN 47403
www.balboapress.com
1-(877) 407-4847

Because of the dynamic nature of the Internet, any web addresses or links contained in this book may have changed since publication and may no longer be valid. The views expressed in this work are solely those of the author and do not necessarily reflect the views of the publisher, and the publisher hereby disclaims any responsibility for them.

The author of this book does not dispense medical advice or prescribe the use of any technique as a form of treatment for physical, emotional, or medical problems without the advice of a physician, either directly or indirectly. The intent of the author is only to offer information of a general nature to help you in your quest for emotional and spiritual well-being. In the event you use any of the information in this book for yourself, which is your constitutional right, the author and the publisher assume no responsibility for your actions.

Any people depicted in stock imagery provided by Thinkstock are models, and such images are being used for illustrative purposes only.
Certain stock imagery © Thinkstock.

Printed in the United States of America

Balboa Press rev. date: 12/6/2011

Endorsements

"So much has been written about transformation, but Waukena Cuyjet's handbook Activating The Power Within is a breathe of fresh air and a must read for anybody who has ever felt not good enough, or worthy to have unlimited good in their lives. Evoking the echoes of Ken Keyes, classic, Handbook to Higher Consciousness, Cuyjet's work offers deep insights, personal stories and exercises that befit her status as a superb teacher of consciousness. It is a book to be savored, not simply read, and a wonderful guide for any seeking the personal transformation of an inspired life".

-   Ernest D. Chu, author of the international bestseller, Soul Currency, spiritual teacher of personal transformation, the creation of spiritual abundance and financial empowerment.

"Waukena Cuyjet bravely shares her own story while helping others find their individual power. She's truly passionate about living an authentic life and speaking her own truth. As a respected spiritual leader in the community, she actively lives what she teaches in this book. The ideas presented in Activating the Power Within can change your life."

-   Leslie C. Halpern, author of Passionate About Their Work: 151 Celebrities, Artists, and Experts on Creativity

Acknowledgments

Many thanks to Christiane Sagnard, my devoted friend for over twenty-five years and editor. Thank you to all my family and friends who were there to advise and listen, staying quiet as I moved through life on my personal journey. I found that they were there for me at every turn.

Thanks to Jake and Tinkerbell, my two rescued dogs, who continually remind me of the joy of giving and receiving unconditional love.

Dedicated to my children

Alex, Steven, and Cecily

Patience, Wisdom, and Courage

Get Ready My Soul

I'm Diving In

Daniel Nahmod

Introduction

I found my power the day I realized I was giving it away every time I let someone or something else do my thinking for me. It was a subtle loss of power, like a new home gradually settling over time. I found that I lived my life based on what others thought, not what I thought. Like you tighten the parts in a new house that loosen with time, I would read another self-help book, attend a seminar, or take a class because I was seeking something. I was convinced that the something I searched for was going to fix me. All I got was a temporary high and some inspiration to take the next step. What I know now is that I didn't need another class. Sure, classes are beneficial for those seeking growth. They also help you stay focused on your life's purpose in today's fast-paced world.

When you are empowered, you are more enthusiastic about your life. You have healthier relationships and experience more success because you are following your heart. Are you giving your power away? Is fear of speaking your truth holding you back? I grew up letting others define me. Something that I should have been embracing proudly didn't happen. It spread like a disease, taking over my mind and body throughout the years and creating depression, sleeplessness, food cravings, and the use of alcohol and shopping to numb my anxiety.

I complained to friends, who listened to me patiently as I shared the drama in my life with them. The one question a particularly devoted friend kept asking me was, "To whom did I give my power?" I was asked this question over a period of months before I really heard it. I had no answer at the time, because I was a know-it-all. Like most professional complainers, I wasn't looking for an answer. I blamed all my problems on what I thought was missing in my life—an identity. I was so sure that if I didn't have to spend time thinking about what race I belonged to, why I didn't have straight hair like my mother's, or why the color of my skin was not lighter, I surely wouldn't be in the predicaments in which I found myself more than once. All I wanted was to know whether I was black, or not. Ambiguous answers were all I got from my parents and extended family members. Feeling like an outsider, I was living with a victim's consciousness.

I wrote *Activating the Power Within* because I wanted to share with you how my life was transformed and how you, too, can empower yourself and create the life you want. I was confused about being Native American and African American, but my feelings can apply to anyone struggling with an identity about whether they are an Asian American, Italian American, Irish American, Arab American, or part of the LGBT community.

Feelings of inferiority will keep you from having and being all that you can. I was ignorant of my God essence. Learning that we are one with God, I know who I am, and that I am never disconnected from Its presence. That's what this book is all about: transforming from feeling inferior to feeling empowered.

When writing this book, I looked up confidence and empowerment, and discovered that confidence in yourself is the most important thing you can have. If you don't have confidence in yourself, no one will have confidence in you. To be empowered, you must connect to your higher self and take charge of your life.

I became empowered when I accepted that something in me knew what to do and I got out of the way and allowed it to happen.

When I was giving my power away, I couldn't express myself, believing I was not entitled to speak my truth even when I knew something was not feeling right; however, I didn't always know what that "something" was. Once I got the courage to act in spite of my fear, I became empowered.

This book is a handbook that is intended to take you by the hand and help you overcome the barriers that keep you feeling powerless. While I share my personal path to empowerment, there will be something that you can relate to.

In addition, this book is intended to be an introduction, or perhaps a re-introduction, to a power within you that you have available to you all the time. Answers to life's questions always come by way of you. That is because you already have the answers to every question about life inside of you. I didn't learn that until I was in my forties and I am still learning it.

I've read that fear of falling and loud noises are the only two fears inherent in humans. When we think we are afraid of something, it is a learned response, and, like all behaviors, it can be changed. All thoughts have a frequency. Fear and love each have a different frequency. What you want and what you don't want are at different frequencies. What you get when you are empowered are cohesive frequencies, allowing you to live a more balanced life.

The most powerful tool you have to energize your mind, body, and spirit is to know that your life is a direct reflection of your internal thoughts. In other words, you must be conscious of what you want internally in order to experience it externally.

At first, I focused only on the need to have a clear identity. I thought all I needed was to feel connected. I only wanted to know, *Who am I?* By that, I meant, *What is my nationality?* One may obsess that being thin or having a successful career is all that is important in life. I knew just by looking in the mirror that I was different. I never felt like I belonged to any race, and I wanted and believed I needed an answer in order to move forward. This question started to demand an answer while I was still in elementary school. I remember wanting to be Italian, like most of the other students were. I remember feeling good when I was mistaken as a particular schoolmate in our class picture. She was from Sicily, and we had the same skin tone and thick hair. Even her mother mistook me for her own daughter.

When I was a teenager, I wanted to have straight hair and lighter skin like my fellow Jack and Jill members. Jack and Jill was a private, exclusive social club where you needed to know the "right" people to be a member. At the time, the club was predominantly made up of people who were not black or white, but instead fell into that category of "colored," which included many shades. Acknowledging a Native American ancestry was not all that important then. I grew up where there was "them," and there was "us." Most of us were solidly middle-class and lived in a certain area of Philadelphia. Since I could not afford to live in that area, I was allowed membership into the club because of who I was related to. Classmates from school and playmates were white and black children. But, once I became a teenager, my social life was only with fellow members of the club.

Even belonging to a group of people who looked like me, my perception of myself was so distorted that I became stagnant in my psychological growth. I pretended to be a part of whatever group I was accepted in.

On my senior class trips to Washington DC and Virginia, I was with classmates touring George Washington's house in

Mount. Vernon when a boy announced, "Let's play jungle bunnies." Not knowing what he meant, I didn't say or do anything. But the other white students looked at me for any reaction. When, after a moment of silence, my best friend in high school simply stated, "She's one of us. It's okay," that was my first experience of feeling powerless. I gave up my power to a classmate.

Activating the power within will introduce you to your higher self in a new context, with emphasis upon the great idea of the divine in you.

It's easy to say "get empowered," but it's essential to have a sense of confidence in yourself to truly be empowered. There is something inside each one of us that is a powerful force. Throughout my journey, I learned to stop seeking things outside of myself. I spent many years wanting an answer to a question I repeatedly asked my parents, "What am I?" I didn't look like my classmates. I didn't look like my playmates. I was taught that "the white man" would either accept or reject me. More so, it seemed as though others just viewed me as Negro, a term used at the time. The Negro I refer to is what the white majority defined. My color and features, as well as my name, made it difficult for others to come to a quick conclusion about my race. On the other hand, I profoundly reject being identified solely as black only because the US government made a law that states 1 percent black blood makes you black, thereby relegating you to an inferior class also defined by the very same institution. I learned that while I can't control circumstances, I can certainly control how I react to them.

I used to think I had to go live on a mountain or in a faraway place. What I found out is that I don't have to go anywhere to live my truth.

This book tells the story of how I let go of the past and will show you how to do it as well. The past is gone. Let it be. It is what it is. Stop all the drama that comes with living and telling your story. You are stagnating and your energy is being depleted with every visit back to the past. Empower yourself and create the story you want to live.

I soon learned that someone else's opinion was not my reality. After you read this book, you will come to the same conclusion. Affirm that it is possible to live an authentic life every day, freely expressing your truth in every communication and all your thoughts. Set high standards for how you expect to be treated. Say yes to your unfolding potential, and yes to your dreams. Check in with yourself often and ask, *Have I done all that I am capable of doing?*

I had an intervention in my life that was my first lesson in adopting new ways of thinking. Upon visiting the Center for Spiritual Living in Princeton NJ I heard a song written by Jai Josefs that changed my life. One lyric, *I love myself the way I am, there is nothing I need to change*, particularly resonated with me. "You have greatness inside of you," the minister said.

Hearing that song, with its uplifting message reminding me that that my essential nature is one of love, wholeness, and wisdom, propelled me in a new direction about how I want to live my life. I heard the words that empowered me and made them my life's mantra. An awareness of something inside me greater than myself was one of the many "ah-ha" moments I was going to experience with this new way of thinking. For the first time, I felt a real sense of connection, and it wasn't with anyone who was in the room with me that Sunday. It was a connection to myself that I later came to understand and embrace as my higher self. I looked at my life and began to unravel the knot

I created out of my life, and as time passed, the knot in my stomach began to dissolve. I deserve the best that life has to offer, and so do you. Set out to define the purpose of your life and actively begin pursuing it.

I came to a point where I no longer needed anyone to label me; this desire to belong had caused me to feel inferior and less empowered for far too long. I stopped the destructive thinking patterns that had kept me from achieving my goals and quickly realized that having control of your destiny makes you a happy person.

Finding courage to love myself, as I am, brought me to heights I never thought I could achieve. I surrounded myself with people who inspired and supported me. I read lots of books about the people I admired and wanted to emulate. This gave me the power I needed to believe that I, too, could be or do whatever I wanted. Classes and seminars were viewed in a new light. I attended with the expectation to grow. I no longer had the need to fix myself and started embracing my own truth.

I found empowerment. When I'm confronted with challenges in life, I know they are opportunities for me to expand my spiritual consciousness. I fastened my psychological seat belt and started my ascent to a greater life experience.

I no longer dwell on why I did the things I did. Instead, I celebrate the shift in my thinking. I took charge of my life. I stopped blaming others. I took mental notes and permanently taught my brain how to make the decision to be present and happy in the moment. I deserve to be happy as much as everyone else. Finding this type of self-awareness is simply a matter of recognizing that you are a divine manifestation. It is all about getting out of your own way and allowing the power within you to express itself. Everything I read suggested that I get toxic people out of my life. But I was the main toxin. Every time I compared myself with other people and felt less than, or even better, than them, I created my own toxicity. I stopped the comparisons once I learned to compare the differences in how I was at the time and how God wanted me to be. I immediately began embodying the belief that I was already perfect in God's eyes and began what I call "the cleanse." I started working on daily prayer and meditation, things that taught me how to find my own inner power. Being empowered, I easily aligned myself with people whom I wanted to emulate. When I connected to my higher source, amazing paradigm shifts began to take place in my life.

Changing my behaviors and my patterns of thinking empowered me. Saying yes to life, yes to my unfolding potential, and yes to my dreams opened doors and made it possible to work toward manifesting anything I desired. Changing my personal history and setting goals that challenged me was empowering and made me willing to take risks in order to grow.

When you read this book, you will want to digest it and utilize what you learn about empowerment. You will want to jump right into doing the exercises. No matter where you are on your confidence scale, you will be enticed to go higher. Even if you do not wish to try something suggested in this book, get the most for your money by using the tools outlined. Dare to have a paradigm shift in your life.

After running six marathons, running in fifty races at age fifty in one year, completing a year of law school, and earning a master's and bachelor's degree, I am about to pursue a doctorate in quantum healing. I know for sure that I activated a power within me that had been there all along. It happened because the source of my one and only power was always there right inside me. I no longer live for validation. I live in celebration of my life and belonging to the human race. Empowered, I get to celebrate my true self and share my inner gifts and beauty with the world every day.

Week 1

Take Back Your Power

~~~~~~~~~~

"The only thing to fear is fear itself."—Franklin D. Roosevelt

If you are thinking this is a huge step to take in the first week, it is. But, if you don't dive in and empower yourself starting now, you will remain on the sidelines in the game of life. That is where most of us have been thus far. Rethink your whole approach to this game they call life. Get in gear and head for the starting line. You know you want to enjoy the game and reap the rewards of a successful life. I am here to help you dive into thinking about being empowered and stop letting others live your life for you.

Do you have to come to a point of frustration or anger in order to say what's on your mind? I used to think I was the kind of person who freely spoke her mind. But, I learned that my empowerment was coming from a place of hostility. I had to get mad in order to express myself. I worked up enough negative self-talk to convince myself that I deserved something, and demanded it while in a fighting mode. I was no longer afraid to ask, claim, or demand. This left no room for discussion of any kind. If internal arguments precede your outbursts, then you are not coming from an empowered place. Being open and honest about anything was not happening for me. I was too afraid to live my life for me.

I learned early to let others do my thinking for me. I gave away my power to others without a second thought. Something in me knew it wasn't right, but I did nothing about it. I hated myself when I behaved in such a manner. Even worse, as I became an adult, I desperately wanted to be honest and authentic. I believed in "what you see is what you get," but for a long time, masked my real self and put forth what I thought was an acceptable image, all the while living with this anger inside.

Dissolve Fear

Fear steals your power. It is a major obstacle that gets in the way of happiness or greater success. I remember being taught in religion class at an early age that I was unworthy. I was born with Original sin. This belief settled into the very core of my being. If I wasn't worthy, then there was nothing about me that was of any worth. This was my earliest encounter with fear and it resulted in not being able to speak my truth. I did not have a voice, because I misinterpreted what my Catholic teaching meant by being unworthy. It became a road map to being without power in my adult life. In high school, when I expressed a thought, or even a question, that contradicted the teachings of my religion at the time, I was punished and told I needed to be reformed. I became afraid to speak my mind. As I got older and other rules were added to how I was supposed to think, this further cemented the beliefs about myself that were false. Finding out who I was and living it was not an option for me. Fear created a distortion for me and inhibited my ability to deal with learning who I was. So, I became what I thought others wanted me to be. It was impossible for me to become empowered when my reality was so distorted.

Fear will keep you stuck as long as you make it your reality. A joyful, successful life is further and further away from you the longer you live in fear. You can only rise to the level of your greatest fear. But when you accept that fear is not your reality, you can overcome it.

What is fear? I heard the definition of fear used as an acronym: Fear means False Entity Appearing Real. We give life to fear and make it real when we hold on to a fearful emotion. Empowered people are ones who no longer hold on to or react with, a strong, fearful emotion when they have an anxious thought. My ah-ha moment came after several months of being afraid of a boss who continually spoke to me like I was a child. Every Monday, I dreaded going into a meeting where I was subjected to his way of speaking to me. After reading some material and spending some time studying how to better honor myself, I went into the meeting a different person. One Monday, as I began my day getting ready for the office, I started to observe my feelings of dread about attending the meeting. I realized that during my studying and reading, I had started embodying what I was learning. There was a process taking place out of my control that affected change in me. I spoke my truth that I didn't like how I was being talked to. I felt a new feeling, one that was not fear, as I went into the meeting. I became empowered when I started observing my thoughts rather than staying absorbed in them. I transformed from my fearful self into the powerful one.

I entered the room a new person. During the meeting, another comment was made that I felt was condescending to me. I went to my boss and asked for a minute to speak with him in his office. I spoke my mind politely, calmly, and sincerely, claiming I would not accept being spoken to as a child. He responded apologetically and I left. He never spoke to me again in that manner. Returning to my office, I felt empowered. Mind you, I had wanted to say this to him long before it actually took place. I learned, from my reading and studying, to believe that I was responsible for my experiences and free to reclaim my power. After that, I became stronger and braver. During the encounter with my boss, I trembled like a captured bird. But, the act of claiming my power was so strong and felt so right that, for the first time, I felt in control. I was not angry or hostile at all. I knew how I wanted to experience my life and acted upon it. All I did was claim my power. I have always given respect to others and I was now demanding respect for myself. I tapped into my higher self the moment I began observing my thoughts. What resulted was a newfound freedom. I spent the rest of the day letting the empowered me get in touch with my empowered self. I created a new road map for my life.

Do you find that you oftentimes say or do what others want to hear or will approve of? If you communicate from that place, you are giving your power away. The more you do, the further away you get from living your truth. I used to imagine that if I were nice to others, they would like me. I had to learn that if anyone was going to like me, it had to start with me liking myself. This often shows up as a disagreement with someone. In healthy relationships, each member of the relationship is being honest and upfront with the other. There are times when you don't say what you want because you don't want to upset anyone. When you pretend that everything is alright, you are giving your power to the behavior, which is the same as giving it to another person. And if you're in a group where no one is acknowledging the unhealthy behavior, you have a group dynamic that is powerless. I observed this in social settings and at family gatherings. Guests arrived and were greeted with open arms and kisses when only minutes before they had been talked about not being wanted at the event. Not accepting the unwanted guests required other family members to be honest about how they felt. This didn't happen, because as a group they were powerless. Instead they all gave their power to the unwanted guests.

Making a decision

I realized that I could make choices. I could make choices in every moment of my life on every subject, especially when it came to me. Each time I made the choice to speak my truth, my confidence grew. I was following my inner guidance, whose only interest is my well-being. I was no longer thriving, I was living.

What is this power of choice? You have the capability to deliberately refuse to entertain any negative thought, so it follows that you can choose to be open and honest all the time. It takes loving oneself and believing that you are worthy. Acting upon those feelings and inviting those emotions into your life builds confidence. Once you decide to assume responsibility and authority for yourself, a lot of things in your life will change. Making the decision to live your truth is the most important decision you can make in taking back your power.

When I said, with as much conviction as I could, that I realized how important this life is to me, I knew that going forward I was going to live an empowered life. When I decided that, things began to change. When I decided to take responsibility for myself, honor myself and speak my truth, things just changed for the better. When I began seriously studying what this life means to me and what my role in it is, I embarked on a path that allowed me to create more joy and love in my life. I had studied for about four years when I learned what the tools were that empowered me. I put up a rock of resistance, because I was a fighter and my way of doing things was comfortable to me. I deliberately moved out of my comfort zone, but I was kicking all the way. While attending a workshop called "Why Aren't You a Millionaire?," I heard the speaker say, "We all have the power to choose. And if you are not a millionaire, you made that choice." I heard that concept and applied it to other areas of my life, like my trouble with making decisions for myself. The brightness in the light at the end of the tunnel went up a notch. It was then that I realized that if it was going to happen, it was up to me and no one else. I was putting lots of energy into figuring out what was wrong with me. Then, I began to realize that there was nothing wrong with me. I learned that I have the power to make choices in every area of my life. After years of feeling generally bad about myself, my world, and my family, I made the choice to live peacefully, first with myself, and then with others. I learned that my integrity and personal values needed to come together. I decided to move forward and really put my faith into being able to create joy, peace, and anything else I desired in my life.

I began to focus only on what was right and good about me. I had been thinking one way about myself for a long time. It took work for me to start thinking about how okay I actually was. My feelings were something I had to work on. My mind knew the truth about me: that I was an adequate and powerful being. I had a voice, and my opinion was important. I had to learn that by virtue of being born I was enough. My old beliefs about myself confused me. My new belief that I was okay became my dominant thought. My emotions said I was not, and that struggle went on for some time.

Eventually, my mind became redirected. I came into alignment with my feelings and my beliefs. Now, I'm free. I feel free. It was hard-earned, but I was worth it. I have my life. Before, other people all had a piece of my life. I had given it away.

As I understood more about this new way of thinking, I really began to have a true sense of who I was in this world. I stopped letting my personal fears keep me from being authentic.

Fear becomes you when you dwell upon it. As I mentioned above, you give it life. Question your insecurities when they arise. Tell yourself that you are capable of anything you set your mind to do. You empower yourself when you change the negative self-talk to the positive and rely upon your faith to know it is so. Learn from each experience and keep going. The universe is here to support you. Align yourself with who you are and you will not fail on this journey. Choose to speak your truth on your terms and in your own timeframe. Fear doesn't stand a chance in holding you back when you choose. Empowerment comes from action taken from an honest place. When you come from the heart, you are never wrong.

Every time you refrain from saying what's on your mind, there is that fear inside holding you back, and you give your power away. Each time that happens, you sabotage your life by not listening to your inner voice. All those suppressed thoughts have to find some place to go. They can manifest themselves as a nagging backache, for example. They often show up as depression, physical illness, or both. The symptoms of pain that manifested in my body ceased to exist once I owned my voice. And they returned every time I forgot to speak my truth. When you listen to your inner voice and speak your truth, your life changes in a powerful way. We all have an inner voice that speaks to us. It nudges us to say or do something about the things we ignore when we are not living authentically. It is essential that you claim your power to choose. Embrace the belief and the decision will become the fact.

You are adequate

Being afraid to express yourself is rooted in a feeling of inadequacy. You have to overcome the fear of speaking your truth if you are to be empowered. Look for ways to free the chains that bind you. Ask yourself if you are always comparing yourself to others. People who participate in this kind of activity can't find it within themselves to speak their truth. You never measure up, because you are judging another in the hopes of finding them inferior.

You are beating the drum of powerlessness every time you do not speak your truth. There are several ways you convince yourself that your behavior reflects the truth of who you are. These are all lies, because your fear causes you to falsely believe that anger gives you the courage—or what you thought was courage—to live. You are not empowered. You are just angry. Your thinking is erroneous. Comparing yourself to others becomes a habitual thought process. It's merely a conditioned response to your environment. When you own your voice, you own your life.

In my household during the fifties, we never discussed what our ethnic origin was in the company of outsiders. Instead, we let others, (teachers, bosses, and neighbors), decide for us. Others always defined us, accepting or rejecting us. Because of my looks and name, I was always asked to define who I was. When I asked my mother what our ethnic origin was, the answer I always got was "other." I was never clearly informed about what my ethnic origin was. It was always about what others interpreted us not to be. My mother believed that acceptance from others brought opportunities that determined one's success in life. That was in the fifties and sixties, when tolerance of other races was at a low. I'm still aware of those old habitual thoughts when asked about the origin of my name, but I respond differently now. Instead of getting angry at the person for asking me a personal question, or feeling vulnerable because it triggers up a feeling of "less than," I now remember who I am. I take back my power by getting out of judgment and into love. It doesn't have to be your ethnic origin. It could be your gender, your job, or your social status. You are judged in many ways by others. It's up to you to stop being a slave to their approval.

I learned that I was made from the divine. It was hard to accept at first, but when I accepted it I began to see myself differently. I am a creative life of the universe. Whatever is in the infinite, I must be in the finite. I no longer had a low self-image. Once you embrace your perfection in your imperfection, there is the joyous acceptance of self. In that consciousness, you can recognize those times when you are giving your power away and pull it back.

Empowerment depends on how you feel about yourself. Whatever you think about yourself reflects itself in your life. Having a good self-image is the most important thing to achieving one's full potential.

Come to know the truth about who you are and your life will change. I recognized early on in my studies that I wanted to change my way of thinking and did so. When you question your fears and the source of your feelings of inadequacy, you begin to empower yourself.

Thinking intelligently about your own life and who you are is what it's all about. Evaluate why you feel insecure in certain situations and around certain people. Come to know that you are special. Accept that you are unique and divine. Everyone is an expression of God or whatever you believe to be the creator of this universe. It's up to you to embrace your truth, the truth that you are a divine creation expressed as a human being. As such, you are entitled to the best life you can live. Your responsibility is not to allow anything or anyone to tell you differently.

Once I stopped striking out at my own bad self-image, I moved into a better place. I hung around people who believed that I was okay. I studied the principles of philosophers, especially Ernest Holmes, and applied them to my daily life. Others didn't see me as inadequate and I became what I wanted to be. I became aware that most problems I had came from poor self-image. When you get to the truth about who you really are, your life changes. If you don't feel worthy because your self-image is low, you cannot have an empowered life. Sometimes, because of a low self-image, you get close to success and then you quit. All that is not feeling worthy about yourself. I went to school, then on to college, then on to law school, then on to graduate school, hoping that one day I would feel adequate. I accumulated degrees, awards, and certificates of completion, always looking for more. During those years of school and my subsequent career, I was critical, tearing down others' success because it made me feel better. Internal work has to take place in order to overcome these feelings of inferiority. Understanding that God is seeking to express itself in you, as you, and through you, helps you become empowered. Life is so much better when you are empowered, and good things start to happen.

Whenever you are caught up in fear and low self-image, you will find that any decision you make from that place, which is not real thinking, and any actions you take, will lead you to try to protect yourself. What you say will not be your truth. It will be only what you need to say to protect yourself. Since that is not the divine expressing itself through you, it must be something from the past. Something your mother or father or authority figure taught you to be. Ask yourself, *Who is doing the thinking here?* At once, you will become aware of the higher self that is your empowered self. When you surrender to your higher-thinking self, you allow the divine to express itself through you. Identify what is making you feel powerless, knowing that in this place, the one thing you can instantly change is your emotion. By becoming calm, you have built yourself a command center.

Tapping into your inner guidance lifts you beyond the life of confusion about who you are and clears your belief. You become empowered by the energy of your inner source. Do what you can to be calm and centered and release the powerlessness that is imprisoning you. Let go and participate in what you want your life to be by speaking up in little ways. Trust the process.

You no longer think that you cannot say what you want when you want to. You no longer give in to what others want to hear. Being empowered is about having a good self-image, a strong belief in a higher power and an acceptance that you are enough. A good way to begin building your power is by befriending your higher self.

There is a myth that there are limiting forces greater than yourself. There is no force known greater than yourself. You were made in the image and likeness of the highest. You come from the infinite; therefore, there is nothing limiting about you. In other words, there is a higher power that is living through you and as you, and any time you think that someone or something out there can stop you, you give your power away. Take that power back and walk with the dignity of your creator.

You can begin to change your mind about yourself. Self-esteem is the opinion you have about yourself. It's that basic feeling that helps you accomplish things. If your opinion hasn't been so good about yourself, get clear right now about how you can change that opinion. By virtue of your birth you have a s special place in this world. Begin by loving yourself. Today can be a special day for you. Turn on the switch that lets you know that you can have a better life, that things can be different for you, because the truth is, you are powerful.

Exercise for Week One

⋏   This week, start doing a regular reality check and identify what your fear is the next time you get that gnawing feeling in the pit of your stomach. If you can't identify what your fear is, look and see what gives you stress in your life. Try to remember when that fear started. If you can't, recognize that it is with you right now and prepare to release it by asking yourself, *If this fear I'm feeling came true today, what will happen?* Know that nothing will happen, because that fear is not real and you can't get something from nothing. It is only a figment of your imagination stemming from an illusion of an experience that you interpret to be real. Living in fear is merely a mismanagement of your negative imagination.

⋏   Remember each day that you are more than your looks, your emotions, and your experiences. You are a spiritual being having a human experience.

⋏   Decide to know yourself as pure intelligence always acting intelligently.

⋏   Practice empowerment. It is an inside job.

⋏   Take a leap of faith and live your true purpose. It is a lot easier than you think. Take small steps.

Week 2

Saying Good-bye to Old Beliefs

~~~~~~~~~~~~~~~~~~~~~~~~~~~~

"If you do what you've always done, you'll get what you've always gotten."—Anonymous

The window of illusion is shattered when you realize that the beliefs you've been holding on to are not the truth of who you are. Sometime in your life you may have been told or made to feel that you are not good enough. Whatever untruths you remember hearing, you must realize that nothing is real to you unless you make it real. Most of us have barriers of some kind or another from the past that get in the way of our happiness. Learning the truth of who you are is your first step in activating your power. What keeps you experiencing the same old stuff are old beliefs, usually passed down through generations, that you have accepted as truth.

Once you embody who you really are (your truth), you become empowered to create new beliefs that serve you. As you make decisions from this new place of authority, more good unfolds in your life immediately, because your experiences are mirror images of your new beliefs. Your reality has to change to reflect your new awareness. That's the way the universe works.

For years, I believed that I was not good enough. I held on to an old belief for many years that I was flawed because of my color. To not be of the Caucasian race meant that I did not measure up to the standards set by society. My immediate and extended family supported this false belief by setting high standards for behavior and education. All of this was to cover up our color. While nothing is wrong with wanting to achieve the best in life, especially when raising children, it is inherently oppressive to be in an environment where you are judged by your color and not by your character. Continuous, negative beliefs about oneself are propagated. Carrying those negative beliefs for years delayed me in getting to a positive place. Ideas were created by my parents and their friends to feel good about themselves. There were times when we believed we were better than blacks and whites. Becoming an adult didn't change that belief held in my subconscious. In the fifties and sixties, almost all people of authority were Caucasian. My reality was that I was a member of the "weaker sex," in addition to thinking I was inferior to others. The belief of being inferior dictated my behavior.

My journey out of the bondage of these old beliefs meant facing the shadows of early childhood cultural oppressions. The more I got in touch with who I was, the chains of old messages embedded in my subconscious mind unlocked. Looking at what was stopping me from feeling good about myself was really coming from inside, not from the outside. It no longer made sense to me to believe everything I was told. It was time to update my belief library. In order to do that I knew I must take action.

Clean out the subconscious mind

Your subconscious mind is a giant storage bin and a powerful part of your consciousness. Everything you experience and all your beliefs are stored in your subconscious mind. The miracle power of the subconscious mind is like a best friend living long distance with whom you rarely get in touch but, when you do, it is like you just spoke yesterday. What makes it a miracle power is that the subconscious mind not only receives what you think and feel, it mirrors back to you exactly what you put into it. Everything you accept as truth is kept. I believed I was less than others and people showed up to treat me that way. Once I eradicated that belief in my subconscious mind, my life became empowered. Learning how to use the subconscious mind opened the door to liberty and happiness

In order to change what you accept to be true about yourself, start pulling yourself back to your essential self. Get in touch with what you may call source, the non-physical you, the divine self, spirit, or God. Whatever you name it does not matter. Know that it is the "higher you" available to use all the time. Calling it your inner guidance or inner voice may help you to listen for answers. Know that there is something greater than the physical you that is wise and is here for you. All you have to do is tap into your higher self. There, you will find a constant supply of God's embodied presence. You gain the power to adopt new beliefs, because knowing who you are empowers you. Your old reality is changed and you begin to express your new reality.

Ralph Waldo Emerson said that "what lies before us, what lies behind us, and what lies around us is nothing compared to what lies within us."

Stop the "I should" or "I ought to" talk

Do you repeatedly say "I should" and "I ought to" when you really don't want to do whatever it is you are stating that you should or ought to do? Words like these are about following rules made for you and are buried deep into your subconscious. They are not about you creating what you want. Living by "I should" or "ought to do or be" rarely, if ever, matches what you desire. I believed in those rules for a very long time. I thought living by those rules guaranteed me a good life. It might make you good, but it will not make you an empowered person. And who was it that set those rules? Those are abstract. Have you ever heard who "they" were? I was always told to make sure to wear clean underwear and have no holes in my socks in case I got hurt and had to go to the hospital. When I was a teenager, I asked my mother one day who made that rule and she replied, "they did." When I asked who "they" were, she couldn't tell me. If you often find yourself on any given day saying "I should," decide now to take one day and become mindful of every time you say a word that requires you to "be" or "do" something. Practice listening to yourself, especially when you are saying "I can't" while you are thinking *I want*. Then, observe how often the next word after "should" is something you don't want to do or be. Check in with how you are feeling and see how it is working for you. It won't feel good, because you are not being empowered when you say "I should" do or be anything. That's when you are making a decision from an old belief that no longer serves you. Also, find some quiet time or place where you can meditate or pray to release those old habits. Bless old beliefs, then release them. If you prefer moving, then take a long walk alone. Let your mind drift. With practice, you can guide your thoughts to create new beliefs that will demonstrate what you desire to experience. A belief is a thought you keep thinking.

Becoming aware of how you think and feel about what you believe marks the end of a chapter in your life. You have to get out of the old story and into your empowered self in order to begin creating your experiences. As an empowered being, you are the director of your life. When the sixties riots began and the black power movement rose, I got into the whole Afro look and wore red, black, and green colors to show my black pride. I played the role perfectly, even though I possessed features that were not African American. I chose to believe what I read in the history books and saw the victimization of the black race on television for myself. That was not my true reality then, and it isn't now. But it justified my drama, my story. And when my black friends at Princeton told me I was not black enough it didn't alter what I believed. What drama are you acting out based on your old beliefs?

Every time an old belief creates drama, redo the scene like the actor does until it is right. Change the "I should" to "I want." Your empowered self is present and aware of what you believe and speaks from that powerful place. Otherwise, you stay unempowered and exist in a fictional drama. You were created to express your desires with all the tools necessary already within you. Learn the simple techniques of impressing your subconscious mind with new beliefs and watch your powerful self unfold easily.

Dig up those hidden beliefs

The bad news is that everyone has hidden beliefs that are limiting. However, we can uncover them and create new beliefs that empower us to have unlimited potential show up in our experiences. To live an empowered life, you must be willing to discover those hidden beliefs. You also must be committed to claiming the truth about how you feel about them. You are not always conscious of all that you believe. I had a teacher who said that if you want to know what you think and what you believe, look at what you have. Take stock of what your life is like and you'll know what belief system you are holding onto. How you speak and the words you use, especially unconsciously, reflect what you believe. Can you accept a compliment? Or are you one of those people who, when receiving a compliment on something they are wearing, reduce the compliment after saying "thank you" with a comment like "Oh, this old thing." If so, somewhere in you there is the belief that you do not deserve compliments. An empowered person is sure of his or her self and receives praise with ease.

What you say and what you think both contain hidden beliefs. Self-talk is another way to express your old beliefs. You may engage in an internal dialogue when looking in the mirror and think you are too fat or your hair is thinning. These negative thoughts come from beliefs you hold inside, and, as you speak or think them, you are confirming their truth about you. Start listening to what you have going on internally and hear what you say to others. Once you identify these statements and feelings associated with them, you are empowered to choose otherwise and reclaim your truth. Even some old beliefs that many continue to accept as true have since been proven false. But, we hold on to them by not being aware of what we say or think.

I worked for a corporation in New Jersey and New York that transferred my office to Florida. I was pleased with this move since I had intended to retire to Florida. Shortly after, about six years later, I was in a meeting one afternoon and experienced something similar to an out-of-body experience. I'd arrived late to the meeting, something I had started to do because I was feeling reluctant to attend them. I was no longer happy working for the company, but grateful for the opportunities it brought me. The available seat was at the opposite head of the table across from my manager. In my mind, I saw myself above the table looking down at it. I heard myself say "My work is done here." I moved through the phases to prepare to leave and left the job approximately six months later. I made the choice from a place of empowerment and was at peace with my decision. When I had feelings of guilt that I was not being loyal to the company (after all, they moved me and my husband to Florida), I was coming from the old belief that you stayed at a job until you were too old to work or they laid you off. I was taught that first you got a good education and then you got a good job. That was success, and you appreciated your lot in life. There was no discussion as to whether you enjoyed your work or not. You stayed at your place of employment and gave it your best. Happiness and satisfaction were not things you achieved. Meditating on what was true for me at the time led to my decision to leave. I made my plans and was ready to go on to the next adventure. My departure was also influenced also by the fact that I was in and out of doctors' offices treating the pain that overtook my body. I went through all kinds of tests and the doctors found that, although my hips were deteriorating from running and from age, the insurance company would not approve a hip replacement. My pain expressed in my hips and down my legs. More tests were done. Physical therapy was ordered and pain medicine prescribed. This time, I was tested to rule out diseases, starting with bone cancer. I was unhappy at my job but scared to leave because of the belief that you stay at a good job forever. In the meantime, I was counseling others to follow their joy. It came to me one day that the only choice I had was to take painkillers, perhaps for the rest of my life, or leave my place of employment as soon as I reached retirement age. I hadn't thought about the fact that in a little more than a year after deciding to leave, I was reaching retirement age. Empowered by my new belief that I did not have to continue to be at a place where I was unhappy, I continued on the retirement path. And so I experienced a life in the corporate world, a successful one for the majority of years, while I enjoyed my work.

The most important way for you to empower yourself is to be aware of your hidden beliefs so you can consciously choose to change them and live an empowered life.

Affirm your new beliefs

Affirmations are a way to align your truth with your new beliefs. Through affirmations, you use words and statements that affect the mind in powerful ways. All the power in your affirmations is yours if you claim it. Saying or writing affirmations daily attract to you what you want to experience. That's the way the universe works. You empower yourself by taking charge of your thoughts and create beliefs that serve you. You have the power already to create and believe what you want. You have everything you need to fulfill your destiny right now. Old beliefs are instilled in your minds by family, religion, even the countries where you live. As adults, you can create affirmations that dissolve what you no longer believe.

You are free to believe what you want with confidence. Holding on to old beliefs limits you and puts you in a self-defeating mindset. When you use affirmations, you empower your thinking, thereby making better choices. When you speak the words "I now believe," you are speaking positively to a new belief. However, if you are feeling fear or discomfort as you say your affirmations, you are speaking with a limited belief. You cannot say yes to spirit and yes to fear at the same time. You must put the feeling behind the words you use in your affirmations. Every time you affirm a new truth with positive feelings, you release any memory you are holding on to that does not align with that truth. In time, the vibration you feel around what you don't want grows smaller and then enlarges as you become aligned with what you do want to experience. Getting yourself into your best-feeling vibration allows you to easily rewire your thinking.

Your best days are not behind you, they are in front of you. Get rid of your low expectations that you have about yourself easily by empowering yourself with positive statements that affirm who you are.

There are no limits to what you can accomplish if you believe that you can and believe that you have what it takes. Believe that you are a treasure, that you have a gift to give to the world. Old beliefs may have kept you down or soured your outlook. Someone may once have said "no" to you, but keep affirming what you desire until you get to "yes." This mental attitude will attract what you want to you. Choose to believe that you are not limited in any way. Use the wonderful power of choice that is inherently yours. Erase any idea that you failed and remove any doubt of your own power. Affirm what you want to experience. Believe it. See it.

You attract what you think about. Where attention goes, energy flows. There is value in letting go of what happened even five minutes ago if it does not serve you.

If not, all you're doing is repeating history. You must come to know who you are right now and what you believe to be true for you. Until you do, you will continue to have the same experiences show up in your life. Beliefs you have, whether true or false, are primarily cultural and societal in nature. As long as you hold off from creating new beliefs that serve you, you continue to produce the same effects. You live a powerless existence because you are letting other people's beliefs dictate your choices.

You are infinite potential. There are no limits to what you can accomplish. There is no reason for you to struggle to get where you want to be. Command yourself to make choices from your powerful self, thereby making powering decisions. Stop the emotional pain that surfaces from choices made from false beliefs. When you give your attention, vision and focus to something you want and add emotion and belief to it, you shall have it. Once you see the results that come from releasing old beliefs, you will never question the validity of your inner power that you are tapping into. Recognize that you can't fix the past but you can start something new. Start creating. Connect with yourself. Be your powerful self. Enjoy your life. Love who you are and bless who you were. Welcome the new, empowered you. Until you do the work and connect to your higher self, you will not give yourself a chance to create a new belief system. Connect to higher power and you transcend the past. When you do, you embrace a power of infinite good. Everything you do, say, and think will be stimulated by truth. Know you are the guardian of your mind. Master ideas for loving yourself. Be directed by wisdom. Be conscious and mindful to feed only seeds of thought you want to grow and expand in your life.

Exercise for Week Two

⅄ Find the trigger that awakens you to your truth and incorporate it into a daily ritual that will help to ground you in your new beliefs.

⅄ Focus on an expanded consciousness and be aware of how you withdraw from your old reality into the many dimensions of reality that you are now aware you inhabit.

⅄ Trust and follow your own inner guidance and watch as you experience a new, exhilarating sense of power, freedom, and joy.

⅄ Spend time in nature and revitalize and replenish your energy. Go where you find it most attractive. When you encounter the beauty in nature, you also connect with the majesty, vastness, and beauty that reflects inside you.

⅄ Make a point of sensing the real beliefs behind the speech and actions of yourself and others.

⅄ Write down three positive qualities that you have and upon reviewing these qualities, know that these are your truths and your gifts to the world.

Week 3

What's Your Mental Activity?

~~~~~~~~~~~~~~~~

"Change your thinking, change your life."—Ernest Holmes

While there is only one mind, it has several distinctive characteristics; the subjective and the objective mind, and the conscious and subconscious mind. Your conscious mind actively chooses thoughts. The subconscious, or subjective, mind receives these thoughts. What you experience in life is a result of what you are thinking. It's the subjective, subconscious mind that responds to the thoughts it is fed by the conscious mind. When you change what you think in the conscious mind, the subjective mind responds likewise. It is essential that you change your thinking so that you in essence plant seeds of thought into the subconscious mind about what you want to experience.

Our thoughts are like seeds. What you plant, you harvest. When you become distracted, refocus your attention to the mastery of your mind and you become empowered. You become present and clear. This empowers you so your next thought is whatever you choose to think. When you are conscious in your thinking, you are clearer about the choices you are making. Being awake and being present promotes clear-minded, forward propelling decisions and heart-centered relationships.

The power of the mind is beyond what is written here. But, when you think positive thoughts, you will have positive experiences. If you want to know what you are thinking, look at what you are experiencing. If you know what you want, then adjust your thinking to align with that desire.

Are your thoughts contributing to love or fear? If you are giving thought to some upcoming event with concern for its outcome, you are in fear. In fear, you create anxiety around a situation that is unknown, uncertain, and dangerous to your health. When you are feeling fear of failure, know that it gets in the way of constructive decision-making. Put failure into its proper perspective. Start by changing your thinking about trial and error, understanding that the learning process is a good one.

When you feel fear, embrace it rather than resist it, because the only difference between a brave person and one who is fearful is that the brave person becomes more comfortable with fear as they face it on a regular basis, like a fireman or policeman. Facing the feeling enables you to take power over it and move through it to a better-feeling place. It is about moving from fear to faith and shifting your mental activity. Usually, habitual thoughts of fear are more about your imagination of what might happen. As you change your thoughts from fear to safety, you become empowered.

Shift your thinking

When living in fear, you live in resistance. The next time you feel afraid, shift your thinking. Attempt to monitor your self-talk, too. Look at whatever it is from a different angle and your experience is guaranteed to change. Wayne Dyer said, "If you change the way you look at things, the things you look at change." Getting yourself into your best-feeling vibration allows you to easily rewire your thinking. That is the way life works. Stop rehearsing catastrophic scenarios. When you stay in fear or anxiety in the face of uncertainty, coping is more difficult and your stress level will increase. Enter a state of stillness and stay there, no matter how uncomfortable it feels. Oftentimes, checking in with how you are feeling tells you what you are thinking. Does your body feel stressed and uptight, or is it relaxed? Training your mind by purposely thinking positive thoughts halts your non-directed thinking. You are no longer unconsciously and uninvolved in the creation process.

Positive thoughts are the key that unlock any door that bars you from an empowered life. Every thought you have, creates. Empowered thinking raises your spirit and activates that infinite strength within you so you can achieve everything you want. Empowered mental activity requires daily practice and mental discipline. If you want more of something, focus on it. Put your mind toward the new experience and away from the current thought. Before you can become, you have to think it. When you think positive thoughts, you step into action. Thinking of yourself as loving, prosperous, or healthy results in behavior changes. Decide to rewire your brain for lasting happiness. In order to do this, you must be conscious of your thoughts.

All habits are formed by doing the same thing over and over, and you ultimately go on autopilot because your mind has been trained to do so. If your thoughts are negative, you are not in the flow. You need to wake up and be present to what occupies your mind. Conscious awareness of what is going on in your mind empowers you to shift to thoughts that are positive. Other people and the things that happen to us in life are not inherently unpleasant. Rather, it is the self-talk about them that is unpleasant. The next time you think you are not happy about something that has happened to you, ask yourself what you can do to change it. Remember, the thought is only as bad as you make it. Remove the blocks of old thinking. They only hold you back, slow you down and limit your ability to live an empowered life. Acknowledge the inner critic that derails your attempts to achieve and accomplish what you want. Look at these inner blocks carefully. Then, lovingly release the hold they have on you. You are merely shifting your way of thinking. It doesn't have to be a big paradigm shift. A slight shift in thinking will open up new insights.

Based on the principle of the Law of Attraction, your intangible thought becomes a tangible experience. Getting yourself into a better feeling vibration enables you to easily reprogram your thinking. You become aware of the thoughts you think and the words you speak. You are the guardian of your mind. It is up to you to take charge of what occupies it. Start by staying aware of where you put your attention.

It is easy to remain in the same thought patterns. You are on autopilot throughout most of the day. Even when you think it is not working, it is, because you will experience exactly what you are thinking.

Create Power Thoughts

We live in an awakened age. We create our thoughts, ideas, and ways of being. You have a voice inside your head. There is a mental dialogue going on all the time talking about what you should do or what you forgot to do. When you step outside of the conversation going on inside your head, you empower yourself and create powerful thoughts. You always become what you think about most. Observe this mental voice and become friends with it. It's never going away, so you might as well make it work for you.

The only way you can stop this excess chatter is to step back and notice it. Become the one who notices the voice, not the voice itself. This is where you become empowered and take over your mind's activity.

When you are consciously aware of what you are thinking, you must make sure that your thoughts are affirming life, not negating it. When you are thinking negatively, you are not thinking along the lines of infinite truth. You create a circle of negative thoughts that are fed from outside influences. You've no doubt heard the phrase, "what goes around, comes around." When you think affirmatively, you align with your truth and expand unlimited experiences. You create a circuit of good energy that comes from within. Your experiences reflect that good energy within and return to you multiplied.

The more you think, the more you have to think; the more you create things to think about, the more exhausting it gets when these thoughts are more often negative. In order to experience positive change and alignment in your life, you must clear your inner environment: your mind. You decide what happens to you. If you are not living the way you want, then you must stop what you are thinking. You are the only one who can change your thinking. It is not easy because your thoughts are addictive and concentrated on themselves. If you don't pay attention, they go in any direction except where you want them to go. As you become more aware, you carefully choose the thoughts you allow in and how you are going to store them. It is important that you keep your mind clear of disempowering habits of thought. Detoxify your mind by stopping the automatic thinking. You do this by becoming the one who is listening and observing the one who is doing the thinking. Power is in the observer, not the observed.

Thinking is part of the creation process and is powered by your directed thought. To direct your thoughts, you need to be conscious of what you are thinking. When you are in your mind, you are conscious. When you are not in your mind, you are unconscious. Thinking is where the seat of your power is, so you need to be in your mind as often as possible. How do you know when your mind is not supporting you and when you are not in control of it? You know it immediately after becoming consciously aware that you have had wandering thoughts. Thinking about what you were thinking makes you feel anxious or worried. You entered into your drama and not in your truth. Your thinking will take you away from where you want to go. To be centered in your awareness, you have to stay conscious. You have to step away from your negative thoughts to see them clearly and do something about it. Decide to be your infinite self and not your ego self.

Empowered living is like a wedding feast. You are supposed to be at the party. You are the invited guest. You were given this life and all the opportunities to live it joyfully. When did you last enter the divine mind and participate in the feast of life? Have you responded to the invitation to joy and abundance? Or, are you one of the guests who turn down the invitation with excuses? Have you just chosen to stay in a mind filled with negative thinking? Life gives you what you expect. Whatever you are expecting, you are experiencing it right now.

Tapping into your higher consciousness activates the power that reigns above all your negative thinking. All thought is creative because all thought creates. Making the connection with "as you think, so you are," you learn to release whatever is keeping you in the negative state of mind. This power is present for you all the time. Give thanks for it. Use it as your mantra until you change your thinking. When you change your mind, you get centered into the foundation of your being. Remind yourself that the love of spirit is saturating your mind. Bless the negative thoughts and let them go. You become powerful by connecting with your higher self. Your thoughts are either uplifting you or dragging you down. Spirit is expressing itself through you. You are here so spirit can express itself and it does, in your form. You are a point of power that has no circumference.

Power of Quiet

Stilling the mind, if only for a few minutes, has a calming effect. It allows you to focus and gives you time for contemplation and meditation on what matters most. It takes a powerful mind to shut down all the mental activity going on inside. This is more difficult when there is so much going on around you. But, the strength it takes to quiet the mind is already within us and we need only to activate it. Look and you will find it. You empower yourself by going within to quiet the mind. You create more power as you sit in the quiet mind.

All it takes is making the time to sit still every day. Do it. If you only have fifteen minutes a day, be courageous enough to go against the stream. Use your power to rise above the bedlam of activity taking place all around you. As you practice this quiet time, not thinking about your day or checking your email, you will become more at ease in stillness. It can be in the morning, after work, or before bedtime. If you need to be outside in a park, or at the beach, or on a path in the woods, make it your priority some time in your day, and you will start to look forward to it. It will no longer be a part of your "to do" list. With practice, it becomes you.

Finding power is not about looking outside of you. All your power is right where you are, no matter where that is.

I started practicing meditation years ago. I still sometimes find my thoughts drifting. They don't last as long and I'm able to come back to stillness and silence more quickly. At first, I used the timer on my oven. I began with only five minutes. In the beginning, I spent the entire five minutes thinking about meditating when my mind wasn't drifting to other things. After I was able to do five minutes, I moved to ten, and finally thirty, minutes a day. Now I do an hour a day. I tried stillness, then mantras, then music. Now I upload a meditation onto my iPod and will not let a day go by without meditating. You don't have to do an hour. And you don't have to get in any particular position except what is comfortable for you. You empower yourself by spending some time in your day in silence, training your mind.

Attitude makes all the difference

Are you one of those people who are always complaining and griping? It is time to stop it. There is always something you can find to complain about, but all you get is more reason to complain. The Law of Attraction will give you exactly what you focus on. When problems arise, you have two choices. You can accept things and continue thinking that life is unfair. Or, you can see it as a challenge to grow. Life is always giving you opportunities to grow. If you didn't get the job you wanted, see it as an opportunity to have a new beginning. Your attitude is what makes the difference in how you experience life. Finding something positive in every situation empowers you emotionally. If you can be grateful for the very thing you are complaining about, you will see the good in it.

Being optimistic is a powerful tool. When you view everything that happens to you as good, you empower yourself to take the next step. Give up your victim mindset and take full responsibility for everything that happens in your life. Ask yourself next time something doesn't turn out the way you wanted, *What part did I play in that happening?* You are a powerful person and the results of the actions you take, whether positive or negative, always show up in your life. When you recognize that, your attitude about what you thought or did changes you from being a victim to becoming proactive. This attitude pushes you into the right action. See the event as something that gives you some power to change, rather than a failure that makes you feel powerless. Look for the seed of something better, especially when everything is going wrong.

I had a boss who stressed me out whenever I was around him or thought about him. I tensed up in the parking lot before going into the office every time I saw his car there. It got progressively worse. I began making errors in my work that were the direct result of my negative thoughts about him. After reading that God is present everywhere and in everyone, I decided to see God in my boss. I chose to look for the good in the situation. It took a lot of positive thinking on my part, but I stuck with it and noticed in time that I was no longer stressed in the parking lot or the office. About three or four months after I changed my feelings and thoughts about this boss, his boss called me into her office. She told me that my boss was being transferred out of our department. My reaction surprised me the most. She, too, was surprised, because I never missed an opportunity to tell her my story and how miserable I was working for him. I had no reaction. It didn't faze me at all. Because I had already shifted my thinking about the situation, I empowered myself to have stress-free days at work. Changing my attitude helped me long before the situation changed. The mind is so powerful if you use it in a positive way. You have the ability to make your life unfold exactly the way you want it.

Tune in to yourself

Empower your mental activity by giving attention to your inner voice. Learn to listen correctly. Be able to listen, and you will hear what you need and increase your wisdom. Commit to the practice of being consistent. You might begin hearing a word several times throughout the day. Spirit gets our attention in whatever form we are able to receive the message.

Also, listen to the way you speak to yourself. Change negative thinking to positive thoughts. Taking control of your thoughts empowers you to listen to the voice and easily direct it. Be one with the emotions behind the way you speak to yourself. Tune in to what is being said and make sure that your self-talk is helping you to succeed and be all that you can be. What you say to yourself sets the tone of your day and your life. The way you speak to yourself is the way you speak to the world.

Be aware of the way you speak to others. If you listen to the way you speak to yourself, you will always be speaking empowered to others. You will be honoring the other person by the way you speak to them, and in doing so, you honor yourself. Being able to do it requires you to have a strong sense of self, to be balanced, and to have integrity. You are present and truly listening to the other person. You are a powerful listening presence always honoring yourself and others.

Listening from an empowered state is the greatest investment you can make. You change your life around when you come from an empowered mental state.

Lessons for Week 3

⅄   Practice working with your inner voice in directing your thoughts

⅄   Take note as to how often you catch yourself with rambling thoughts

⅄   Sit in silence for at least five minutes each day and notice how your mind wanders

⅄   Start your day with a positive thought and take note when it changes to a negative one

⅄   Immediately direct your thoughts to something positive

⅄   Plan your day and work your plan, addressing issues as soon as they arise

⅄   Turn your listening ability around by tuning in to your inner voice without judgment

Week 4

Remembering Your Purpose

~~~~~~~~~~~~~~~~~~~~~~~~~~~~~

"It is the mind that makes the body." —*Sojourner Truth*

Wisdom and intelligence are always revealing themselves to you. They embody your very being. You don't have to create it or manufacture this. You only come to know it. That is your purpose: to know who you are in relation to this power.

By understanding that you are an individualization of this power, you are on your way to waking up and remembering your purpose. This power is wisdom, and it is conscious of itself. As you evolve spiritually, you discover that its presence is constant. It does not compromise itself from any bargaining on your part. It is order. It is all-knowing, omniscient, omnipotent, and omnipresent. Through the practice of study, affirmative prayer, and meditation, you gain insight into this power. You are the image and likeness of this presence. You reflect and reveal its nature. You have the same qualities as this power. You may not be expressing them in your life, but they are always, always within you. You are the very essence of power. As you become spiritually mature, you become more aware of who you are. Being spiritual is discovering the ultimate source of meaning and happiness within yourself: love.

You learn by expanding your consciousness into the limitless possibilities that are yours. Your core values embrace the desire to be transformed and you become a beneficial presence on the planet. You are a member of a community that is based on unity, wisdom, spirituality, and love. As you travel on this lifelong journey of discovering yourself, you connect to this power. The power responds to you by corresponding to its own nature in you. As you vibrate at a higher consciousness, you demonstrate outwardly the power that is within you.

The truth of your being

Life is not always smooth sailing, but it is your life. What you make of it is up to you. You did not come on this earth to blow with the wind. You were born with an intelligence to use.

In my home, I was told what my purpose was. After getting a college education, I was to marry and have children. I could study to become a teacher or a nurse. It was in my thirties, married and with three children, enjoying my life as a mother and wife, when I began reflecting that my purpose was to do or be more than what I was currently experiencing. I had thought my purpose in life was fulfilled. Then, I returned to school to get more degrees. I entered a field where I worked hard to get promotions and more money. All the while looking for fulfillment, I thought I had found what was missing in order to feel whole. My life was fulfilled because I chose my lifestyle, or so I thought. However, I was following the rules of others. I interpreted my desire to succeed as a parent and an employee as living my truth. It did not fill the void inside that asked the question, *Why am I here?* I was not connected to the truth of my being. Becoming aware that I have access to a power that is available to me, I activated the presence in my life. I gained insight into truth and participated in the unfolding of my life.

I learned that all I desire is liberation, and seeing the truth of who I am showed me what liberation is.

It is up to you to know what the truth of your being is. You are not here to serve others by following their rules. It is your nature to be kind and compassionate. But you don't have to live your life according to others' rules. You are set free when you know the truth of your being. You no longer look to achievements for the purpose of your life. You learn that you have to do nothing to tap into infinite joy and peace. When you internalize your oneness with power, you trust your inner wisdom and find unlimited ways to express your truth. Check in to see if you are trying to fill a void in your life with something frivolous that has nothing to do with your soul. Stop and be still. Know that there is a presence and a power that is within you.

There are many stories told about how you came into this world. Regardless of how you learned how you came to be, understand that the purpose of creation is for God as you know it to express itself as you. Whatever you believe your life's purpose is, the one thing you are to do is experience joy, peace, love, and success. Success is living your truth and letting the rewards of the presence manifest themselves in your life.

You are power; therefore, you are empowered every time you remember the truth of your being, because you come to the realization that you are unique and an unlimited being of spirit. Embrace the knowledge that there is a power operating within you that knows what to do, how to do it, and when to do it. Let this power work in you by becoming aware of its magnificence and live your purpose by being one with it.

Know your life is worth living

If good things are not happening in your life naturally, it is time to create a new paradigm. You can have more out of life and elevate the quality of your life by empowering yourself. Once you surrender to your higher self and get out of the rut of thinking that where you are is all there is, you become empowered. Instead of going deeper within where our power is, we get stuck in frustration, resentment, or anger over what our life has become. When you surrender your lower life to the higher, you begin to see and feel the unlimited power of spirit. A life that is worth living is a surrendered life. You no longer have to control the outcome of your life; you trust the journey. You are not surrendering to a presence that is judgmental. You surrender to a divine order that you depend on and welcome into your life. This process allows life itself to have its way with you, and you come to the understanding that you have been inhibiting life based on your perceptions of a duality, creating your life based on those limiting projections. As you let go and become one with the power of God, or whatever you call your power, your old idea of life begins to disintegrate. When you see through duality to unity, a powerful existence with unlimited potential emerges. You step into the land of pure potential where you live with purpose. You discover that there is only one power. Choose to surrender daily to the power through affirmative prayer, meditation, and contemplation, and your life will be transformed beyond your expectations.

Recognizing you are a part of the whole, you take dominion and responsibility for all aspects of your life. You stop judging on the basis of appearances and look for answers that unify and align you with your power.

Changing your idea of a life worth living can seem overwhelming. It doesn't have to be. When you activate the unlimited power within you, it helps you see a better way. When you connect to the source of your power, you become empowered from within. It is from this awareness that your life becomes more compassionate, more loving, and more accepting, and you embody the qualities of a spiritual being.

Unblock the flow

Stop making excuses for how you live your life. At each moment you choose, you either allow things to happen to you or you take control over your life. An empowered person chooses consciously. You are surrounded by a universal, divine presence, and it is there for you to use. If your life doesn't flow the way you want it to, perhaps you have chosen to live in terms of pleasing, rather than terms of being. When you are in the flow, you live your life without resistance. You act in spite of the appearance of fear. When you live in the flow, you objectively observe your behavior without judgment. You are empowered to forgive until there is nothing left to forgive. You know that there is a greater idea that transcends what is before you.

Living in the flow empowers you by giving you the freedom and happiness you seek. You make all your choices consciously and know that all is well in your world. Your emotional life stays in balance. Your life is calm, invigorating, and exciting. You know what a joy it is to be alive and to fulfill your purpose.

Do you know what the hot spots are in your emotional life? When they are triggered, know that you are no longer in the flow. Place your attention toward the spiritual world in which you live, and you will step into "beingness" and out of the condition that occurs in the physical world. You unblock the divine flow when you choose being over doing. Let go of the conditions in your life and let your powerful self surface. Say yes to spirit, for it is here to serve and guide you to infinite joy and happiness. Think about what you are doing. All of your power is with you now. Get into alignment with your spiritual self and let the physical follow. Your power is not in what you do; your power is who you are. Be connected to your power. Release all external concerns and flow through your day empowered by consciously responding to everything that happens to you. You come from a positive and uplifting place of empowerment.

Because you are connected to every role you play, you are opened up to shine your light of love. You are here to release life's energy. Your life unfolds full of love and joy. You radiate these qualities because you are expressing your divine self.

Happiness is right where you are

There is one basic energy empowered by spirit. It is light. Within this light there is love. The more aware you are of your purpose in life, the more love you experience. Awareness is seeing the light. The light that you are is the intelligence of God. Understand that you are created by God and that you have all the power to be happy. You are here to express God as love. Where there is love present, so is joy. Where there is love, fear cannot exist. Love and fear are polar opposites and cannot be housed in the same consciousness. Love is a positive force, while fear is negative.

There are different levels of happiness. Because a condition arises that does not feel good, it does not mean that happiness has disappeared. It can't, as this energy force is more powerful than any thing or any person.

When you feel unhappy, you are only experiencing it. You do not become it. The emotion of unhappiness is temporary and is only felt as long as you give your power to it.

You don't have to work to be happy. In the metaphysical interpretation of "Seek ye first the Kingdom of God and all else is added," there is a valuable life lesson. First, realize that you are the kingdom. It's nothing outside of you. It is saying, "be the kingdom." When you are the kingdom, experiencing yourself as love, everything else is added. As the kingdom, you create love, peace, and magnificence. You create that which you are. If you are one with God, you will experience yourself as heaven. If you are not in a place that appears to be heaven, you are transformed. Happiness is present because you are in love with all life. You are in alignment with the truth of who you are.

The treasure you are given is not a thing. It is a feeling. Happiness appears in your life because you are the kingdom. God expresses itself by giving you the gifts.

Embodiment of your oneness with spirit empowers you to see things differently. You see good everywhere you look. Instead of seeing what you don't have, you see what you do have. You live with gratitude for the house you live in or the car you drive. You continually feel gratitude for what you already have. You are happy in knowing you are abundant. You rest in the knowing that happiness is not a destination.

Meister Eckhart says, "If the only prayer you said in your whole life was, 'thank you,' that would suffice." One of the things that had the biggest effect on my life was the realization of the power of gratitude. I wanted a more expensive car when I was retiring. I saw it in the dealership when I went shopping. I bought the less expensive car because seemed like the wisest thing to do at the time. However, I no sooner left with my new car when I started thinking about the luxuries of the more expensive vehicle. Driving my brand new car with all its many accessories, I only thought about what I didn't buy. Then I heard a lecture about gratitude. Nothing came to mind at first, until someone complimented me on my new car. I immediately became grateful for what I had and accepted my choice. I began a gratitude journal and focused on what I was grateful for, rather than what I was missing. Understanding the Law of Attraction more clearly, I affirmed my abundance until I embodied it. It was about a year later when my husband called me into the computer room, showed me the very car I wanted, and suggested we buy it. In turn, I gave him my new car from the year before because he was in the market for one. Appreciating and recognizing that my life was already good and knowing that I was the kingdom brought me additional opportunities to be happy.

When you unify your consciousness with the omnipotence of God, you become the power of God. Gratitude is a creative force. Whatever you are grateful for becomes your experience. If your happiness depends on money or obtaining things, then you will forever be powerless to the person or entity you are relying upon to give it to you. But if you see happiness as your natural state of being, that you have it by divine right, then, you only have to be still and know. Let your life unfold by divine right order.

Happiness has always been yours, for it is the very essence of the truth of your being. You empower yourself when you consciously choose to be a part of this divine flow of life. Your purpose is to be love, here and now. Learn to express great joy. You have the power to choose how to express all the inner qualities you have.

Looking outside yourself for answers will never bring you joy or happiness. It will never reveal your truth and purpose. When we go to our inner selves, our higher selves will get empowered. We start living according to purpose and to divine plan. We are unfolding the greatness that is at the center core of our being, and that is good. It is there for you, and you are supposed to have it. We cannot say our life is hopeless, that we are helpless, or, that there is nothing we can do. If you ever think those words about yourself, stop at once because it is not the truth. There is always something you can do to make your life better. The power and the presence of spirit do the work if you activate the power within. Stop living with the primal fear that you are not enough. It is not the truth. Look to your emotional life, see where you need to do some work, and be willing to do that work. Return to your power within and get in alignment; get centered. Then, live your life with all the good you can experience. That is your purpose.

Exercises for Week 4

⅄   Remember an experience when you recognized a power greater than you or God and record your experience in your journal.

⅄   Journal for a week about your inner journey of spiritual development.

⅄   Look at a condition you want to change and identify the qualities of God that you want to experience.

⅄   Find fifteen minutes this week to meditate on gratitude.

⅄   Visualize living your life in the flow, recognizing that you are already living in the flow and can experience expanded possibilities regarding your gifts.

⅄   Start a gratitude journal.

Week Five

The Gift of Empowerment

~~~~~~~~~~~~~~~~~~~~

"If I am not good to myself, how can I expect anyone else to be good to me?"—Dr. Maya Angelou

Spirit, the omnipotent power, is your sustainer of life. Whatever you call your higher self doesn't matter. Focusing on it and allowing yourself to feel love, connection, and oneness with it, is the greatest gift you can give yourself.

If you don't know your higher self, think about some things that take place around you without the interference or assistance of any human, and you will come to know it. What makes the trees lose their leaves in the fall and grow again in the spring? Or, contemplate how your body heals itself when you scrape your knee or burn yourself. Perhaps you apply an antiseptic and bandage on your child. While you forgot about the scrape and continued on with your day, new skin grew. Once the bandage is off, there is new skin with barely any evidence of a scrape. Those are just some examples that describe this higher power. Look into a mirror and think about the fact that you were once an egg, then an embryo, then a fetus, and now, you see divine order looking back at you. You don't always see it, but the existence of it is embedded in everything you do. If you take the time to connect with it, you have tapped into the inner wellspring of your soul. From your inner reserves, your life is refreshed and revitalized.

To live a powerful existence, you must take time out of your busy life to get rejuvenated. When you withdraw from the routines, demands, and expectations of everyday life, you can connect with your inner self. In the core of you, your soul, and your higher power, is where you find your natural rhythms, the stuff of life that created you and sustains you.

This gift can only be given to you by you. If you ignore yourself for too long, spirit has a way of nudging you into awareness. You have an obligation to take care of you. It is no one else's responsibility. By gifting yourself with love, you also give to those you love.

Loving yourself enough to take care of you, you become empowered and set free, because you have consciously unified with the truth of your being.

I understood early in life that there was something greater than myself, and it wasn't what I was taught about God in school or at church.

When I was at the beach as a little girl, I enjoyed the power of the waves knocking me down. I watched as they also knocked down adults and anything else in their way. That was my first experience knowing the power of God; of seeing God expressing itself. There was no stopping the power of the ocean. I didn't see God as something revengeful or mad, which is what I had been taught . I only saw it operating in the ebb and flow of the waves. To me it was a joyful God playing as water. That power greater than anything I knew was reinforced when I was about eight years old. Hurricane Hazel came through Philadelphia. I remember when I curled up under my mother's sewing machine, I again saw that that there was something more powerful than anything in the world, more powerful than my father, my uncles, my teachers, and even the priests at church. Everyone I thought was powerful was not as powerful as spirit.

I felt connected to spirit. It was a wonderful gift I received in my youth. Even today, hurricanes and storms do not scare me. They serve as a reminder that there is a power greater than any human, and I embrace its presence even when it expresses as a storm.

Get balanced

The essential elements of our being are usually ignored. You stay unaware even when you are waking up to yourself. Two elements of your nature are divinity and humanity. It is only one thing. One is contained within the other. Your divinity contains your humanity. If you remember your humanity is in your divinity, you would remain in balance and not create chaos in your life. Take control and understand. You are infinite divinity expressing yourself as sacred humanity.

Sometimes, you forget your divinity and experience spiritual amnesia. When you do, you identify only with your humanity. And what you believe about yourself, you express. Your ego driven life keeps you off balance. You are in a state of vulnerability and powerlessness.

Get back into the awareness of your infinite self, what you know is your truth.

It is not easy to stay aware and awake when you are unbalanced. Some even express pain in the back or someplace in your body, when you are unbalanced.

You were not an accidental birth. You are much more than what you think you are. You are more than your circumstances or conditions in your life. Whether or not you have been thinking of yourself as a failure or having done horrible and dreadful things, you are a part of the sacred in human form. That is your reality and only that. You can come into balance by thinking differently about yourself. Recognize your true reality. If you think from your higher self, you align with your truth and get back in balance. Spirit created you and wants only to express through you, blessing you. Get yourself out of the humanity self and into spirit. Coming from the ego mind you exist in fear, anxiety and a belief of not being taken care of. You see yourself as a victim; powerless in consciousness. You live in a state of being combatant or defensive.

Are you ready to get in touch with your spiritual self? When you do, you live empowered in balance, in alignment, your human and your divine acting as one.

You live your best life when you know that you are are in balance, fully contained. In this energy field that is all knowing, you think into it whatever you choose. When you do, you manifest a life more powerful than you can imagine.

Get physical

Physical well being encompasses both your body and your mind. Empowerment is having strength, resilience, and the capability of doing or accomplishing something. It includes physical strength and mental strength. When you involve in a physical activity you are strengthening your body to perform in the way you want it. At the same time you are empowering yourself mentally. It is an empowered mind that tells you to go the distance and takes you there.

Being physical no matter what it is or how long you are active, clears emotional and energetic blockages in the many energy fields of the body. It also clears blockages in the subconscious mind. The clearing process empowers you. You rise to a new level of creativity. You go deeper in to your spiritual practice and enhance your own evolution. It doesn't matter where you are on your journey. Getting physical opens the door to forgiveness, unconditional love and self-acceptance, all the ingredients of an empowered life.

Moving the body oxygenates the blood, cleaning out any impurities stored there. You get in touch with a lot of repressed emotions you hold on to and let go of those emotions once and for all. Poor self-care shows up as illness, bad temper, too many commitments, an inability to complete tasks, depression, accidents and above all else, a feeling of powerlessness.

Exercise supplies fuel for your unfoldment. This fuel that strengthens your body directly feeds your spirit. You are here to let yourself unfold. The moment you begin to let your own being express, all negative emotions fade away. You find yourself floating much like the runner's high one gets when the body moves into that space of no time or place. You connect with your higher self and maintain that connection if you participate in daily exercise.

The joy is your fuel. After you complete the physical exercise, you are continuously being fueled with joy exactly like the way your metabolism stays at the higher rate when the body exercises often. It allows you to live your life more inspired, to create from a deeper level. You operate from a higher conscious of self.

If you are already involved in an exercise routine, take it to another level by doing it mindfully knowing that you are divine expressing as the one who is exercising.

If you don't exercise or think you hate the very idea of exercising, begin in the consciousness of loving your body. Then decide to nourish it with movement as you would when you feed it. Honor yourself by caring for your body. If you only take a five minute walk everyday you have empowered yourself the moment you shifted your belief and decided to take care of your body.

I started running when I saw my husband do a marathon. I was so inspired watching the thousands of runners cross the finish line having run twenty-six point two miles. I knew then that I wanted to do it one day. I began walking around my development until I could do a mile. I reported on my progress as though I did a marathon. But little by little I was empowered to do more miles and entered my first race, a mini-marathon, doing a three point one race. My belief that I could do a marathon got stronger every time I ran another race. I started doing longer races and once I completed my first half-marathon, I knew a marathon was in my future for sure. The preparation for every race regardless of the distance was the same. I had to go out and run. I also had to prepare my mind telling myself that I could do it. So six marathons later I watched my spiritual life grow believing more in myself along with my getting to run marathons. The power I felt crossing the finish line after every race is the same power I feel when I remember who I am. Doing something physical allowed me to see in form, what I can only feel in consciousness.

Begin seeing yourself as being more than your physical body. You are more than what appears before you.

No matter what's going on in your life, take time to honor yourself with the gift of physical exercise. You don't have to justify it to anyone. Use your power within and step into the unknown, if taking time for yourself is new or challenging to you. Spend only a few minutes each day, if that is all you have right now.

Get spiritual

Focus on a greater idea than what is known to you now. Dare to expand your spiritual life. Begin with Practicing the Presence. Learn to be more aware of the Oneness. Go to another level of spiritual development. Accepting being with yourself empowers you. When you love yourself right where you are, all negative judgment of how you feel about yourself is removed. Perhaps this moment alone connecting with yourself is new to you. Allow yourself to feel any discomfort that surfaces. Allow yourself to stay present and focused. Decide to open to a new and greater relationship with you and Spirit. It becomes easier to stay awake, to stay present when you strengthen your connection. It is easy to remember who you are when you stay present. It is only natural that you start to see the perfection of life continuously unfolding in you and feel a deeper sense of your divinity.

You enter a place where there is no time or space and easily release all doubt and fear as they do not exist in Spirit. They are seen as an illusion in the greater scheme of things.

What would your life be like more empowered in the way you communicate with others? There is a bigger picture to be seen to be experienced.

A daily one on one consultation with Spirit receiving guidance empowers you to move forward on your journey. Remember you are more than your body, more than your education, your job, your role in life. Create a spiritual practice that feeds your soul.

Get prayerful

Spiritual practices are powerful, energy generating, connection processes that awaken the soul when they are heart centered. Prayer has a major role in maintaining health. Health and healing happen when you maintain a close connection with Spirit. Spirit is the source of all our good and that includes health.

Whether you use words, mantras, chants or rosaries, anytime you are in prayer, connecting with Spirit, you are empowering your mind and body.

Prayer is not a simple affirmation. Real prayer is communion with God. Prayer is not just saying words or making sounds. You enter into a higher vibration of believing, feeling and sensing that the thing that you are praying for is already done. These are the components of positive prayer. You pray without judgment. In Affirmative Prayer you are not supplicating to something or someone outside of yourself. You become empowered when you pray in that zone where you are communing with Spirit.

When you pray, you connect to God also referred to as your higher self, that inhabits your body knowing the perfection and the wholeness that you already are, claiming it so that it shows up in your experience. When you are in prayer you are not separated but are acknowledging the oneness with all life. You can expect to have your prayer answered or demonstrated according to your belief and the embodiment of your belief. You come to an awareness of the omnipresence of Spirit. It unfolds in its time and in its own manner. You allow for the greatness of life to manifest. Live your life prayerfully. Enter into your prayer from your heart and release yourself from your negativity and wake up in the presence of Spirit expressing as you.

Affirmative Prayer in not invoking a presence that you ask God to do something that God would be reluctant to do otherwise. Affirmative Prayer is in contrast to a supplication prayer. Affirmative Prayer affirms that God is good and God is right where we are. Because God is right where you are and God is good, you are entitled to believe in yourself and entitled to imagine that wisdom is working through you, And that Divine wisdom through you is able to address the problems and challenges of life.

So you affirm your goodness and your possibilities and you affirm that God is with you to help you to do all these things. What God does for you God does through you.

I didn't pray daily until I was in my forties. But when I learned how to pray affirmatively, concentrating on positive forces, I received good. I affirmed the absolute truth that God is good.

If you look at the Twenty-third Psalm, it says "God is my shepherd." It is an affirmative prayer. There is the affirming of God's presence. There is a gratitude. There is the connection of the human to the Divine. I learned that my good is always at hand. I found an affirmative prayer in many of the various holy books.

Affirmative prayer was challenging at first when I affirmed health while I was experiencing the flu. But in affirming that the medicine that I was prescribed to take was good, I was restored to health. I retrained my thoughts to understand that God is working through me, the medicine, and through the researcher who made the medicine. I firmly believed that God is good. God is expressing in, as, and through me. I also decided it was the same God that heals me.

For prayer to work, you have to constantly affirm who you are. Look at what you want and believe that it is already yours. The steps of affirmative prayer are to remove any blocks that are present because you are not seeing in your life what already exists. It is the affirming that there is already all good everywhere present, abundance, health, love, and peace etc. Using this scientific method of prayer requires you to become one with what is.

The five steps of spiritual mind treatment created by Ernest Holmes teach you how to get into the vibration of oneness with

Spirit and open you to accepting all the good God has to give. Accepting that it is already present in your life is your key to manifesting your desire. Recognition is the first step and all you are doing is recognizing that there is a power and intelligence everywhere present, including in you. Next is the unification statement, which is you connecting with it. If you stop there and feel the vibration of oneness, your prayer will be answered. You have consciously stepped into the realm of the absolute. No condition is present when you are in the absolute. So there is nothing to be healed.

When you desire a specific result, you do the third step which is the claiming that which is not in your experience is yours by divine right action. Then you show gratitude in what life is expressing right now. The final step which is very important is releasing. Releasing the prayer is letting it go and letting God do what God does. To not release it would be like the farmer who plants a seed and continually digs it up to see if it is growing roots. You cease to discuss or think about your condition that you released.

When I decided to enter into a prayerful life, I ceased relating to some of my friends. This was challenging at first especially when they realize you are no longer the miserable person they used to commiserate with. As I experienced more joy in my life, I gained compassion for them. I did not feel sorry for them as that would be in judgment of them. I came to understand that they did not understand my new positive attitude. Or they didn't want to see it. I even pushed some buttons with my change in attitude.

When you make the commitment to live more prayerfully, you are empowered as to how to be in relationships that are challenging. You easily accept that other people have different ways of doing things. If you find yourself getting disturbed by their behavior, check in with yourself. You are no doubt in judgment and need to do more work.

Change your thinking and change your life is what I was taught when I began my Spiritual journey. It takes courage and initiative to look for the good. And if you don't see it, don't give up, keep looking. It's there. Begin a prayer practice and do it daily. Tap into your power and let your life express perfectly.

Get some time alone

Another gift to yourself is time alone. Time with yourself is an elixir you can use as a daily dose. How nice it would be to take five minutes out of the day and get silent. In the silence there is peace and unspoken joy. You take yourself out of the chaos and noise. Here is where you can find yourself. Where you find you, you find God. Wherever you are, God is.

You have these precious moments to observe your thoughts and release any that no longer work for you. Look at what serves your highest and best interest and release those that don't.

There are so many times when you are caught up in family duties, or a have a commute to a job, or maybe you are relied upon by a relative who needs you when you are done with your regular obligations. You want to take time for you even more.

Five minutes of silence can calm your mind and empower you to deal with things from a different perspective. When you take control of your time, you take control of your life.

Until you take time for yourself everyday, learn who you are, connect to your higher power, you will stay the person you are right now. And if you already are an empowered person, then I invite you to take it up a notch. You empower yourself when you see who you are and honor yourself by becoming emotionally and spiritually full and balanced.

Even if you just walk around town or drive your car alone, you've entered silence. Observing your surroundings setting your attention so that it is fixed, you would unknowingly remain silent. Your power of thinking would develop further thus empowering you when you do speak.

Lessons for Week 5

⅄   What great thing would you give your life to if you were absolutely assured of success?

⅄   Put your attention on something for five minutes and observe how the silence feels

⅄   Write down your three favorite aspects of your life today

⅄   Write down three of your challenges in your life today

⅄   Write a Recognition statement and a Unification statement as your prayer

⅄   Name two things that when you participate in them, time dissipates

Week 6

Begin Where You Are

~~~~~~~~~~~~~~~~~~

"It isn't until you come to a spiritual understanding of who you are—not necessarily a religious feeling, but deep down, the spirit within - that you can begin to take control." —Oprah Winfrey

To achieve real empowerment, you need to be confident and at peace with every part of you. The hardest part of getting started is to just do it. Celebrate that you desire to be more than you are right where you are. Honor your journey and the courage it takes for you to go deeper into self-contemplation. You must have some reason for wanting to become empowered or more empowered. Perhaps you experienced some kind of discontent with yourself, or you experienced feeling powerless. Whatever the reason, you are motivated to start. Know that right where you are is okay. Celebrate that you have said "yes" to life. When I attended meetings at the New York Road Runners Club during my trainings for the marathon, the one thing that inspired me the most was that the facilitator said, "if you get to the start at the Verrazano Narrows Bridge in Staten

Island, the first island of five that you will run through, you are already a winner." You are already successful.

You are always in a good place when you are at the beginning. In other words if you don't like where you are in life and want to change, it doesn't matter because becoming cognizant of how you feel, brings you to the beginning of something new. That's good because now you start out knowing what not to do. Therefore, your chances are greater. Whatever you set out to do, you will be successful. And if not, you just come back to the beginning and start again until you get it the way you want it to be. Instead of focusing on everything you disliked about your life, you get more inspired to succeed at what you desire.

In Ernest Holmes's book, *Science of Mind,* he said "wherever you are is your right place." There is no other place better than where you are at the moment. That is your beginning point. He also says that wherever you are, God is.

You may be reading some inspirational books, or joined a spiritual center or started meditation. Wherever you are on our journey is good. It may not feel like a great place at first but, if you believe there is a greater experience beyond what is expressing at the moment, and declare your purpose, you activate your power within. You are starting from a powerful base that can only become stronger.

There is you living in the world among the conditions. And there is the self that knows what to do at all times. Self in new thought terms is about a lower self, human, and a higher self, Divine. The lower self is that part of your psychological nature which deals only with external facts. It appears to be separated from that which is good, perfect and holy. The higher self means the realization of truth; the spiritual man/woman; that which is conscious of its union with goodness, truth, and beauty, that which is always constructive, the empowered you.

So often one goes within, and taps into one's spiritual self, when facing a crisis of some kind, dreaded disease, a divorce or the death of a loved one. You are at a powerless point in your life. Some of you have jumped on the blame game, pointing to others, chose the angry route or became a victim of circumstances. You similarly thought that someone else holds the power. Regardless of what has taken place before now in your life, going forward is not about what happens to you but how you respond to it that matters.

I know from my own experience how painfully easy it can be to simply give up and blame life or other people for my unhappiness. For years, I blamed society for mistreating people of color even when I was not directly mistreated. I blamed my father for not being around to protect me when I was vulnerable to others. I blamed my white friends for rejecting me and my black friends for not accepting me. I was a victim of my circumstances. Then I got angry and went after anyone who got in my way. The worst thing that happened to me is that all the blame, anger, and victimization didn't change my circumstances. Empowerment is something you do to yourself.

I believe that you create your own happiness and unhappiness when you are disconnected. Constantly focusing on what you don't want and fighting against situations and circumstances occurring in your life, you continually live with an inner unrest. When you make the shift, decide to do your life differently, you empower yourself. When that shift happens, you begin a new life. You own your power.

Begin your shift by deciding what personal issues or circumstances you would like to change. Remember you don't need permission to make changes in your life. You can write the things down that you can do today, this week or this month. You have unlimited time. Just begin right where you are. You don't have to take big steps. Lao Tzu says, "A journey of a thousand miles begins with a single step."

Joy of journaling

If you never paid close attention to your life, journaling will open the doors to a new you. It is an invitation to pay close and serious attention to how you are living. When you journal, you capture your inner path of spiritual development. It facilitates your inner growth. Journaling is not just about words anymore. You can capture your path in drawings or adding pictures. What you put in your journal is for your eyes only. You may want to journal about feelings or thoughts that arose during your day. Or you may want to list your "wins" only at the end of the day. Experiment and find what part of the day works for you. Perhaps you will discover you are a reflective writer capturing at the end of your day all that happened and how you felt. It's your book. It's your life. One or two lines a day may be all that you want to capture of that day.

According to research in the JAMA, April 14, 1999, persons suffering from asthma and rheumatoid arthritis significantly reduce symptoms by "Writing about how you feel about stressful life events helps to put things into perspective, expressive writing." Where you go next is benefited by knowing where you have already been. You increase your awareness the more you journal. It is a great place to document thoughts, feelings and even solutions. Writing daily you capture fresh from the heart. Many events occur during your day that inspire you and preserving them in your journal makes them accessible when you want to relive them or be reminded of something pleasant. When journaling, focus on the content so your thoughts and feelings flow unencumbered. You may want to note the date and/or time of your entry.

When I trained for a marathon, I kept a diary of how many miles or how much time I spent running each day. This propelled me to keep up the running at the same time inspiring me to stretch the distance and the time. As I reviewed where I had been, I was empowered to go further. I journaled about the weather conditions for the day and whether I was overheated or too cold. It allowed me to make adjustments on the next run by looking back at what occurred in the past. When I review past entries, I am reminded where I found my power to accomplish such things as the marathon. This is a tool I have when I am out of alignment and need to reconnect with that inner self.

Discover the treasure inside you. Your writing is a transformational tool with the potential of enhancing personal growth. It is a means for self-inquiry and self-discovery. It's inner work and yours to do. It is the work that empowers you by bringing you home to your own truth and where your power resides.

Your intuitive power

Begin by setting your intention to live completely from your inner knowing, your inner heart. As you do this, your consciousness will change as you engage in the power of your intuition. There is something in you that knows. It's your higher self and you have access to act knowingly or even sensing without the use of rational processes. Learning to listen expands your ability to be receptive to what your intuition is directing you to do or say in any situation. Living from your higher self, using your intuitive power, with an open heart takes practice.

Listening to your inner self is a spiritual practice. It shows the way to deepen the inner life and grow in a conscious awareness of your truth. Listen from the heart before you speak as often as you can and you will come from a place of peace, wholeness and power.

When we listen, what we hear is our own guidance, our own wisdom, that still small voice that speaks to us giving us direction. It takes time to develop deep listening. Using our intuitive power we discover ideas, words, peace and certainty as to what to do next. Learning to listen well with the heart you discover that your human self and divine self become one.

You no longer have to look for tools and techniques to improve your life when you develop your intuitive power. Inner communication is a valuable asset. It's value is enhanced as long as you grasp and understand that there is this spiritual energy available to you and you access it.

What would your life look like if you stayed alert and attentive to your inner voice and acted on the inspiration you receive? You will have nothing blocking your mind waiting for some outside stimulation to tell you what to do about it, assuming you are aware of the message coming your way. If not, you would be acting upon someone else's idea to clear up your stuff. And if it doesn't work out, you have only yourself to blame. Trusting your inner guidance and heightening your feelings will make your life flow a lot smoother. Additionally you become sensitive to what hunches you feel another time.

Everyone is born with a natural way of receiving inspiration. Prior to my mother's death I searched for a church. I was looking for answers to questions, some I didn't know yet. I visited many different denominations over the years, but never felt that connection. Every one in some way reminded me of what I knew of religion and I wanted something else. I didn't realize I was on a search to develop my spiritual self. It was nudging me and showed up in all kinds of ways. I lived in a town where I drove up a two lane road to get to my development. It was the only entrance to my development. Before turning left, there was a sign on the right that I saw. It said "Center for Spiritual Living." Later I saw the sign above it that said "Religious Science Center of Princeton." It was the Center for Spiritual Living that piqued my interest. When I was a passenger in the car heading to my home, I stared at the sign until it was out of view. Where I was in consciousness at the time, led me to believe this was a place not for me. Living in a university town, I assumed it was connected to it. The words were what resonated with me. My inner voice said "investigate" while my outer voice said "this is not for you." I didn't have high self-esteem during that time. Eventually, I looked at the telephone number on the sign and committed it to memory. Shortly thereafter I called the number to ask what it was all about. I got the answering machine on my first call and every call thereafter. I didn't hear anything but the invitation to join them on Sunday with the time and what number to press if I needed directions. I left a message asking for information about membership in order to attend. I received a return call on my voice mail cheery as ever with a more hearty welcome to come visit on Sunday. Where I was at the time, the cheery voice piqued my interest even more while at the same time pushed a button of mine. I thought "how could anyone be that happy?" I was led to call one more time with another question about this organization. Every time I passed the sign I was drawn to read it like a magnet. One Sunday I got up and got dressed to attend. I thought I was going to just another church but the cheery voice of the minister who was on the voice mail kept playing over and over in my head. Delaying leaving the house I turned on the computer. I spent many minutes listening to my outer voice that said "no it is only another church" and my inner voice saying "go check it out." I chose my inner voice.

During the weeks leading up to the telephone call and attending my new home, I was taking yoga classes and attending a writing group facilitated by the same person. I really enjoyed this person and probably would have participated in anything she led. When I walked into the service on that delightful Sunday, I recognized her sitting towards the front. She was sitting next to the co-facilitator of the journal writing group I attended. I felt immediately that I had found my new spiritual home. When the music started, the opening song was "I Love Myself the Way I Am." Well, I was so overwhelmed with joy hearing the song, seeing my friend and ultimately meeting the woman with the cheery voice. I learned that day to listen and listen intently when my intuition was guiding me to go somewhere or do something especially when it took me out of my comfort zone. I have been attending Centers for Creative Living, now called Centers for Spiritual Living, since. I am grateful that I followed my inner guidance each step of the way and remained true to myself.

Take small steps

If you find you do nothing while you want to make changes in your life, perhaps you have set too big a task to do at one time. Have a vision of what steps you want to take and make your goal achieving it match that vision. Think about how your vision can come into being. Any size task can be done if reduced to a simple form. Taking small steps works only if you discipline yourself. Begin small steps each day that will help you grow without pain, fear and stress that often come with change. Connect with your inner your power and listen for guidance on how to proceed.

You can ask what must you do first or what must you do next. Then listen. Your inner wisdom will guide you.

Be sensitive and kind to your developing self and break free of old habits that you must act upon a new idea immediately. You did not become the person you are overnight. Transformation takes place through a gentle process of opening the heart and mind to Divine love and consciousness. You are learning how to respond intelligently rather than to react emotionally to events and conditions in your life. Being empowered is being in harmony with all life. Peace comes from being centered and easing into this new way of living. When we achieve a soul connection, the business of living takes place from an empowered you with ease and grace. You are learning how to be more intimate with yourself which means connecting with your feelings in an honest yet respectful nurturing manner. Your work here is a process. You are immersing yourself deeply in the process of becoming empowered and how to connect with it. Using the creative process is getting to know God. Whenever you feel overwhelmed, ask yourself what you have learned about yourself in this process. It might be a place to stop and reflect, contemplate and wait for the next step. Empowering yourself is a process that is becoming conscious of your eternal truth. It unfolds gradually.

Do you remember a time when you set out to do something and planned to stop after a time? And you were going so well that you kept at it until you were exhausted? When that happens you tend not to want to go back to the thing you wanted to do. On this journey you don't have an end time. You are ever evolving and growing.

Practice with doing things differently; regularity is essential to living an empowered life and is essential to your transformational process. Like working out at the gym, you gain muscle and more power the longer you exercise, gradually building the force you put on yourself. You need to create empowering thoughts for yourself that reflect your highest and powerful self.

There is a powerful driving and creative force inside you that, once tapped into, empowers you. Embrace it and live an empowered life taking one step at a time.

Lessons for Week 6

⅄   Listen and observe how it feels to be in alignment with Infinite wisdom.

⅄   Journal your thoughts and pay attention to any feelings that surface

⅄   Make a list when you feel stuck and take one of them and think about what steps you can take to get unstuck

⅄   Write a story of when you listened to your intuition. Be specific about what your inner voice was saying.

⅄   If you journal at night, journal in the morning for one day

⅄   If you journal in the morning, do it in the evening at least once

⅄   Be alert to any answers you may receive to a soul-searching question.

Week 7

Create a Powerful Environment

～～～～～～～～～～

"If you want to know what you are thinking, look at what you have" - unknown

Having an empowered life includes an environment that supports and nourishes you. When you came into this world, you made demands right from the start. When you were hungry you cried. When you were cold, wet, just plain uncomfortable, you cried. And you didn't stop until someone came to you and made your environment pleasing to you.

While you no longer cry when your are uncomfortable and there's likely no one who comes to you to make you feel good again if you should, there are things you can do to create an environment that works for you.

Empowerment is from within. There are no shortcuts to power. It is a process you go through where you awaken to a higher consciousness. You gradually form new habits of behavior including the way you think. Most behaviors are not genetic; they are a product of your early childhood development and life experiences. You can easily form new behaviors.

Empowerment includes what is in your physical world too. Do you surround yourself with empowering people who think powerfully so that you can be nourished and supported in a powerful way? Who you surround yourself with is instrumental in nourishing your environment. How you think can be empowering or it can be dis-empowering. You don't become powerful from certificates, degrees or promotions on the job. You may hold powerful positions, but that does not make you empowered.

Being empowered is not about controlling others. It is an aware person whose level of consciousness transcends conditions and experiences. An empowered person is astute to his or her surroundings and observes them objectively. You respond rather than react to people, places and things.

What your surroundings look like can tell a lot about you. Start with your home and your car as part of your home. The way you feel about your home gives you insight to where you are emotionally; how you decorate it, your furniture, books collections, etc. But, more importantly, "what does it says about you?"

Your vehicle serves as the symbol for progress and movement through life. Too much clutter may represent an inner fear of moving forward, or an inability to let go of the past so you can move more freely into the future. You may be blocking yourself from moving on, not letting go of pain from the past. In other words, are your house and car controlling you? Have you surrendered to your stuff? If you are not self-assured in your home or on the road, you are not in charge of your life. Check to see if your space is in alignment with your purpose.

Physical environment

Your home is supposed to be the most comfortable place to you. If your stuff affects your mood or interferes with your feeling productive, you may be waiting for a mood swing that makes you feel powerful. Don't cheat yourself from growth and expanding your consciousness because you live a cluttered life. A clear mind soon disintegrates in a cluttered home.

What your physical surroundings look like and what relationships you engage in limit or expand you. Your home should be a place where you get energized. Is it a place to relax, quiet the mind, and rejuvenate? If you need to locate something important, can you find it? Consider ways that can make your physical environment empower you. Organize if you must.

Everywhere you look you see messages to simplify your life. There are warnings that if you don't take control of what you own, it will control you. Today, choose to live with intention and set small goals clearing your space. When you decide to toss something out or give it to charity, see yourself as having decided what happens next with the item. You are using your power over your belongings by putting things out there. You participate in the law of circulation and open the avenue to the new every time you choose to discard your stuff.

Your relationships either weaken or strengthen you. If something about your relationship makes you feel powerless and you can't or don't want to change it at this time, you can alter your reality. You do that by remembering your truth. Come from your place of truth. State truthfully what you want out of the relationship but know first what you want. This can be from a spouse, child, significant other, co-workers, or friends. Additionally, they can be a vessel by which you attain empowerment. Healthy communication is the key. What you think of yourself determines what that relationship will be.

If you did nothing else after you were born, you are still special. You are the only treasure worth holding on to. And that does not require you to change. You are here to expand and express. An investment in your state of mind is all it takes. You don't need more things or more accomplishments. What you need is a larger sense of self. Understanding these truths enables you to bring something special to any of your relationships.

How do you create a supportive environment when there are restrictions? If you have only a small space that you can claim yours, do so. A reading corner that you design with nice lighting, a comfortable chair and whatever else makes you feel good about yourself while there. If you can designate an entire room, then do so. Make it your cave or sanctuary. Call it whatever you want but let it be known that it is your space. If none of that is possible, you can move furniture around in a room and generate new energy and even change your perspective. You can think like a child and create your room to foster creativity and positive development. You may find it ignites your imagination too.

Take a look at your car and what do you see? Your car implies more about your life than you think. If you have lots of things stored in your car including empty coffee cups that need to go into the trash, you inhibit your expansion. Your car serves as a symbol for progress and movement through life. When you block yourself with clutter, you block your ability to move forward. You remain stuck right where you are. Anytime you are stuck physically or emotionally from moving forward, you are in a powerless state. Clear out the physical clutter first. Not doing so will continue to make you feel powerless. Check your emotional issues around clutter that caused the clutter in the first place. Empower yourself by taking small steps to creating your powerful environment in your car. It may be an easier place to start than your home. Vision what you would want your car to look like if, every time you drove it, it made you feel that you could do anything or go anywhere in the world.

Mental environment

Are you spending your time watching television or movies where you vicariously live someone else's life instead of creating your own. How you use your relaxation time can prevent you from achieving personal mastery as well. Entertainment in any form is relaxing and it gives you time to unwind. But make sure it is not your escape from frustration about where you are headed. You can get wrapped up in someone who is living the kind of life you find yourself wishing to have. When you are empowered you know how to pay attention to yourself. You know how to validate yourself and have a healthy sense of your self-worth. You don't need to live vicariously through some one else. Other people can not fulfill your emotional needs.

When you get thoughts of defeatism, you usually start comparing yourself to somebody else. Stop immediately because all you are doing is stacking the odds against you. It is important that you turn these feelings around. This is especially helpful if you are obsessed with following the successful person on television. You can rid yourself of inadequate feelings on the spot by getting re-centered and think instead that there is no one else like you and that you are unique. You are an individualized expression of Spirit. No one has your fingerprints or your talents. Then look at the positive qualities of others. Watch and learn from other people and emulate great people, but do so only to improve your skill sets.

If others express negative opinions about you, keep in mind that what they say is irrelevant to you. What other people think about you is none of your business. When you are empowered, you consistently meet your own needs and you do not need to have other people's attention. My therapist told me to be the cake and let anyone I form a relationship with be the icing. If you have relationships that do not sweeten your life, then do something about it. Perhaps you are looking for someone to be "your" cake? It's your journey towards continuous improvement and only you can walk your path.

Because personal empowerment comes from inside, you assume responsibility for yourself by becoming informed and focused on what you want to have in your environment. When things aren't as you like them to be, you come to a realization that change is necessary.

Being clear about what you want is important to being empowered. Committing to daily spiritual practices creates a guiding philosophy on how you can direct your life and keeps you on track. You naturally surround yourself with everyone and everything that empowers. You keep at a distance those people and things that make you feel powerless. In time, you will no longer attract people and things that take away from you. Your new environment will always be an addition to your life. It will be the icing on the cake.

Whether you are in a situation that you can't avoid or one that is self-imposed, you can find a supportive environment. You will attract people or things that feed you spiritually and are aligned with your vision.

If people around you are not supportive, and you experience external resistance, be prepared for those people to become less a part of your life as you grow. Often people are uncomfortable to change. They may try to stop your growth, but as you maintain your power about where you are going, they will give up. Your power to move forward cannot be stopped by their stagnation. They are conditioned to how you used to be. You shake their world. They will join you on your journey or get out of your way. Making changes is scarey for some. Know that by your growth you are forcing them out of their comfort zone. They may fear that they are going to lose you and they are right. The old you is being replaced by the new person who has developed integrity, humility, justice and industry. What you can do to overcome this external resistance, is to get very clear in your own mind why you are now accepting yourself as responsible for your own actions, attitude and thought. Then, when you encounter resistance, you will have established your boundaries. You will not allow others to disrespect your boundaries because you will know that saying yes to them is saying no to yourself and doing so you are not in alignment with your truth. Remember the last time you were in a situation where you said yes when you wanted to say no. Let that be a thing of the past and know it is okay to say no. Living in integrity encourages more good things to happen in your life.

Stay in alignment with who you are in every relationship at all times. You have to take care of you before you can take care of anyone else. You always have a choice. You become the example and an inspiration to others as you grow.

If people are not physically available, you can create your own support group. Napoleon Hill calls them your Mastermind group. Select five people you admire whether dead or alive. They can be former presidents or scientists. Read everything you can about them. Next time a problem arises, you can ask yourself "what would these people do?" Pick out people whom you want to emulate, who inspire you. People who would make you feel honored to be in their company.

As you progress and you make a commitment to be empowered, you will attract like-minded people locally. Join a book group where the books you like are being read. If you find none, start one. Commit to finding one person you align with and commit to supporting each other. Share each other's ideas, goals and dreams and you will attract more like-minded people into your environment. That's how the Law of Attraction works for you.

Continually believing in yourself, will have immediate results. Emotionally independent self-empowerment techniques allow you to discharge anything opposing your new beliefs. It becomes easier to succeed at whatever you want. Have a plan of action that creates a deeper connection to God. Listen as you are guided by your intuition to recognize you already have an environment that empowers you. You empower your environment when you give direction to your life and determine its course of action. Make a decision now to accomplish your goals in a consciousness of power and love. Commit to letting the Infinite Intelligence direct you. Be honest with yourself and willingly admit and release all judgments and negative emotions. Claim your power now. Use the powerful resources you already possess. Tap into your internal strength and you will accomplish what you want in every area of your life. Overcome any fear and eliminate anything that stops you consciously and unconsciously.

You can change anything with the right mind set and then move into action. Condition yourself for empowerment. Step into an unstoppable momentum inherently yours by nature of your Divine self and unleash the power within.

When you are authentic, you are energized. Embrace your attributes and celebrate you. Empowering your environment is a natural next step in your personal growth.

Clutter should be my middle name. I had things in every place imaginable. Some I could identify and some I couldn't. For a few years I extended my clutter to a storage place where I paid twenty dollars a month to keep my stuff. I had only a faint idea of what was in there. It was my emotional attachment to them that got me to pay money so I could keep them. For years I held onto papers from college and supplies from any activity I was involved in. As a result, I spent time going through all that stuff to find what I needed.

I attended a workshop where the assignment was to get rid of the old to make room for the new. I realized when I got upset doing my assignment that my identity had been tied to those papers and books. My worth was what I accomplished. When I got to the assignment to accept myself as I am, I was able to release all of those items. They were kept for my ego. I continually needed more and more things to make me feel good. Feeding the ego requires a lot of work whereas living from my truth is just being. My biggest burden was carrying around a false belief. I relied on what I did rather than on who I am. I felt I had to do something of importance or significance in order to be a person of value. And after every achievement I went on to the next because the ego never gets satiated. Although my awards, diplomas, certificates were out of sight, I waited for the next search through my worn out papers to feel whole. I defined my existence by what I had accomplished.

I grew up believing that I was not good enough. So I lived many of my adult years proving I was by taking classes. All my efforts were focused on searching, accumulating and achieving in the hope of finding me and being comfortable with me. There's nothing wrong with attaining degrees and awards but make sure you are expanding and not grabbing for something to make you whole.

Learning to trust your higher self, the search is over. Know that you are enough. Accepting this as your truth, you expand your consciousness and no longer contract it. It is in that space that you can easily release the mental and physical clutter in your life.

If you are hanging on to papers or anything that you use to feel good about yourself, you are living from a false sense of self. One of the great things in life is that we can change. You are destined to walk the path of power.

Lessons for Week 7

⅄   Take one thing out of your car every time you leave it

⅄   List five people you most admire and read something about them

⅄   Next challenge that arises try to look at it objectively and not respond emotionally

⅄   Find one thing you are attached to because it makes you feel important and throw it away

⅄   Give some of your old clothes to a charity

⅄   Celebrate what you have in your home that empowers you.

Week 8

A Life without Limitations

~~~~~~~~~~~~~~~~~~~~~~~~~~

"Life consists not in holding good cards but in playing those you hold well."—Josh Billings

Empowering yourself is the journey out of limited living and into greater existence. Every day is lived in the consciousness of Oneness with Spirit. Empowerment means having a personal vision about how you intend to live your life. The process involves rearranging your neurological patterning. You are no longer your thoughts. You observe your thoughts. You are not your emotions but you feel your emotions.

You claim your Divine right to experience happiness and to be successful. You are thankful for everything. You have the power to accept who you are and to love who you are. You trust your higher self, and become one with the ever-present indwelling of the Spirit expressing itself as you. You give yourself permission and the right to decide what to reject and what to retain. Stepping out of your comfort zone no longer meets with resistance. You embrace the opportunity because you know it is a way for you to grow.

You life is approached from a very different perspective when you come from empowerment. Deciding to improve yourself is a natural undertaking. You realize that you can and want to be all that you can. Those who desire empowerment, develop patience, a commitment to living their truth and staying connected with their higher self. Know that you are always supported and have the wisdom of knowing that everything you need is already yours waiting to be activated. There are innumerous opportunities before you to continue on your journey. It is not about being in control of your life. It shows up as a disciplined life. What does this look and feel like? Unlimited living is about being authentic, living with confidence and passion.

Authentic living

One of the most powerful truths about you is your authenticity. Being authentic is about the quality of always being in truth. It is the integration of your beliefs and how you live. What you say, do, think and intend are in alignment. No longer do you have to be anyone other than yourself. There is nothing to prove; only the acknowledgment that what you are is good enough. Your choices are not determined by other people's expectations. Knowing what that is, you freely experience each day in peace and harmony with all life. You wake up, find deeper meaning and live your truth. Your loyalty to yourself is to remain in integrity.

You have finally met up with the urge in you that knows there is more to life than what you are experiencing. You are drawn to explore what that is. No longer are you interested in staying where you are. Your uniqueness is demanding to be expressed. You can taste it, you can smell it. It is closer to you than your very breath. You know what you need to change in your life and move forward. You give and receive unconditional love comfortably. You feel safe and trusting because you have found a quieter voice inside. You are wise as to how Spirit works in your life. There is no need to be defensive. Accepting everything as energy, you allow everything positive and not positive to pass through you. It no longer finds a home in your consciousness to come up again and again when triggered. You are free. You have your own expectations and design your life to meet them.

You approach every day ready and enthused about what path you choose, claiming your rightful heritage to an empowered life. You are at the doorway crossing the threshold into a life like no other known by you before. You live passionately, and confidently.

You may not feel authentic all the time. But you go within and listen until you are centered again. When your experience does not match your desire, you know to choose another path. When some experience finds you at the bottom, you always manage to get up on your feet. There is that part of you that will not stay down. You are backed by a support system that will keep you moving forward. Being one with God you operate at your best.

You have accepted your higher self to guide your way. As you embrace this empowered living, you step into the flow and live each day fully. You have acknowledged your core values and live by them. That is who you are. You have arrived at a place where you know confidence and wisdom in dealing with everyday challenges. You do so with ease and grace. You are living your ideal life each day fulfilled.

Living with passion

Imagine being so inspired that your life reflects the dreams you had in the past. Discovering your passion and making your dreams a reality happens in an empowered life. Everybody has a passion. You owe it to yourself to take time to find out what is yours. It is the key to achieving whatever you want in life and is the reason you accomplish anything worthwhile. When you know what your passion is, you have your vision of how it looks and nothing keeps you from taking action. You walk through your fears focused only on your heart's desire. Following your passion is a journey motivated by you.

You acknowledge each day is a gift and you open it like a present. You set the intention consciously and clearly how you want it to unfold. You carefully unfold your day aligned with spirit. You embrace whatever is before you knowing it is all good. Any challenges are mere pebbles on your path and there is no such thing as an obstacle you cannot overcome. You see every event as energy and observe how it flows through you accepting every experience as an opportunity to expand. Living your passion means that whenever you are faced with a choice or a decision, you will always choose in favor of your passion. You know when asking yourself if the choice you are about to make brings you closer to your passion, the answer will lie within and reveal itself to you. Staying in alignment with your passion, your dreams manifest always. You rely on your inner guidance to take care of the how for you know it is not your concern. Your job ends once you listen to your heart and follow it.

Like minded people are drawn to you and support you in every way. They want to be around you because you make them feel good about themselves. You are the spark. You are a very powerful creator and you grasp that truth. You are the one to shape your life.

You recognize that you are not living your passion when you feel bored. You do some deep searching within yourself and allow Spirit to reveal to you what you need to do in order to realign with your passion. Being empowered, you know what your passion is. You feel happy in how you spend your time each day. You do not look to money or other things for your happiness. Knowing that you can't have long-lasting success in life just doing something well and for a long time, an empowered person learns what he or she loves to do and does it. You embrace your natural high because you are doing what you want to, what you are called to do.

Living with enthusiasm

Your daily actions bring more joy, excitement, delight, love or whatever you define as enthusiasm into everything you do. It cannot be contained. It is contagious and desirable. Others will want to capture and bottle your enthusiasm; you bring energy into everything you do. You are never bored. Being empowered means you have enthusiasm as your objective and success automatically follows. You know that you can achieve anything important to you. You have the opportunity to choose enthusiasm every day. When you live enthusiastically, you resolve to be a better person putting all of your effort into doing so. When things look grim, you know to act as if they are better and you soon will experience it. It's not just about being hopeful when things are in the dark. It is about remembering that the light of life never stops shining and you can see it when you shift your thinking. You live in the present never worrying about the future for you realize that as you pay attention to living well now, you set the stage for what you want to experience tomorrow.

Being self-assured is your natural asset. You are able to totally immerse yourself in what you want. A healthy image is the basis of self-esteem. As an empowered person you experience a life expressing as confidence and a high self-image. Positive self-image is about seeing doing and being exactly what you want whenever you want. Believe in your ideal self and you will step into living an unlimited life.

In being at peace with who you are, you have achieved a sense of freedom. You accept the fact that you have what it takes to do whatever is before you. Your consciousness is awakened and an awakened consciousness enables you to see who you really are and release any attachment to limited beliefs about your capabilities. You are happy and contented and sure of yourself in directing your life. No longer are you concerned with how others think you should be or what you should do. You bless the people who presented challenges in your life and are very thankful to them for reminding you who you truly are. You build your self-esteem by recognizing that you are a spiritual being in this universe.

Being spiritually empowered equips you with a positive energy. You see yourself as a powerful being. You have created an environment that supports you. You focus on what you want your life to look like and not on what happened to you in the past. Right now is what is important.

Living as love

You are an empire that is ever growing. You show up in life in a bigger way. You know that having a loving relationship begins with loving yourself first.

The emotional and spiritual gift you receive by stepping into your loving self is far more priceless than anything you can purchase. You are a creation of the divine.

Your life is no longer about doing; it is about being. Taking time each day to meditate, being still and quieting the mind allow you to center yourself and keep you in a loving state of being. Seeing yourself as love, you live with unlimited potential. You lovingly express in mind what you want to experience and the Universe mirrors your thought in form. You have discovered your purpose in life and live it. Trusting your inner voice you make all right decisions.

The power of love is infinite in its expression. You are unlimited in how much you give and receive. God as you expresses in many ways. Opening your heart to love, you become a powerful force that is unstoppable. You know your divine existence and you live knowing this truth.

There is a natural state of being that is joy. It is who you are. Everything in your life is an expression of joy even when it appears to not be. You lovingly embrace all challenges as an opportunity to grow. You no longer dwell on the past. As an empowered person, you have a new way of thinking. Living in the present is where you choose to be. Your courage to think differently is with you all the time. You are consistent and focused. Because you are at peace, you easily find common ground and shift the dynamic between you and others. Always understanding your boundaries, you respect them and joyously live in harmony.

Celebrate your path, honor it and rejoice in who you are every moment. What you achieve in life by being true to yourself, is a gift that no one can take away from you.

Love is all there is. Every time you follow your heart you are living in love. Everything you do is a spiritual activity. Why not flow upstream living from a place of empowerment and loving every aspect of your life?

Make that shift by choosing to be who you are. Live your truth and trust the process. As you travel your spiritual path empowered, you will progress further on your journey. Continue to activate the power within connecting to your own Higher Self knowing that the guidance and wisdom are always there, always available. Enjoy this amazing trip

I have complete freedom to live life in any and every way I choose, but I also have complete responsibility for every thing I think and do. I am a creative living being, with unlimited powers of life available to me to use for my good.

One day in a Science of Mind class, I heard a fellow student talk of her concern about visiting relatives and she stated how she felt guilty because she did not want to visit her parents on Christmas since she wanted the children to be home to open their presents. She invited her parents to her home but they wanted the family at their home. I related to this because, when my children were young, I set the rule that the children were going to be home every Christmas for this same reason. I paid my parents and in-laws an alternate visit on Christmas Eve. I noticed I didn't relate to her guilt. Bear in mind that I spent most of my twenties and thirties feeling guilty about anything and everything. At that time, I and my circle of friends almost strived to be guilty. As the teacher continued talking about feeling guilty I became aware that guilt was gone from my consciousness. I sat in class trying to remember when it left me. I soon decided it didn't matter. Just enjoy that it is gone. Later that week it became apparent to me that guilt left at the time I began to shift my thinking on living my truth. I lived with acceptance of myself, having learned how to love and honor me. It didn't happen overnight. I was reading books about empowerment. I was on a spiritual journey. On my spiritual journey I was connecting to my inner power, but most importantly I believed God was pleased with me all the time. I understand now how the process worked. It didn't matter when I stopped the guilt trips. I celebrate who I am at the moment.

Empowering myself and have it extended to my relationships required me to shift my thinking about myself. Until you accept yourself you can't accept others. If you see faults in yourself, you are seeing faults in others whether you realize it or not.

Realizing that I am an individualized expression of God and loved unconditionally I have come to accept my perfect self even when I see imperfection. I see my truth instead of my story. When I pass a mirror now, I sometimes see fat in all the wrong places. Sometimes I see my color as drab, hair not so good. But shifting my perspective I have the tools to use. I no longer stray from my spiritual path. There is nothing else I need to do. When I make mistakes, I no longer chide myself or compare myself to others who I claim are better than me. I accept that I am ever evolving and I possess infinite possibilities for my perfect expression of life. All ideas of any negative thoughts about me or about what I say or do are dispelled for I am empowered by Spirit that knows and supports me in changing my thinking. I choose to accept thoughts that are in alignment with my Truth. I get out of my ego by remembering I am Divine having a human experience.

Spirit is always there waiting for me to turn around in my thinking. I show up knowing that I am love and am lovable. I move forward empowered by this truth about myself and let my love express.

Staying motivated

You are more likely to manifest your desires as long as you are motivated. It is all in your attitude. Motivated people have an attitude that is contagious. They are self-starters. Empowered people stay motivated by using tools that they have gathered through study and carry with them all the time. Because they are self-starters they create whatever tools are needed to work for them.

It is easy to stay motivated when all is going well. When things seem challenging and your motivation feels like it is waning, that's when you see the strong and the not so strong go in different directions. You are the one to get yourself going. Again get back on track. The empowered person knows that it is important to call out the forces from within. You have books that are inspirational. There are several videos to watch by motivational speaker who got you going before. You have only to Google the word motivation and you have at your disposal more than enough sites to explore. Do whatever works for you. Sometimes you get motivated after being quiet for a moment. An empowered you will know to stop that distraction and get centered, reconnect to your higher self. You don't have to have a plan on what to do next. Spirit will let you know.

An empowered person knows how to activate it. Once activated, you can evaluate what is standing in your way and begin to move any blocks that surface. Empowered people have strategies in place so there is not a lot of down time. You anchor yourself in your belief focusing on your goal.

You won't find powerful people sitting around a table with others telling their story of how they can't succeed. When you are empowered you know that movement is important. Deciding to get going lets you meet up with your guiding force. You activate your power by just making a conscious decision. Spirit waits upon you and when you get in alignment, it makes the way for you to move forward.

Lesson for week 8

ᚷ Whatever your spiritual practices are, commit to doing them daily

ᚷ Spend one day seeing everything that happens as energy. Allow it to pass through your heart as energy. At the end of the day reflect upon how it felt in your journal

ᚷ Remember that what you think today will be your experience tomorrow. Pay attention to what happens the next day and reflect back on your thoughts the day before. You may want to journal your thoughts of the day the night before. Keep doing it until you see results

ᚷ Meditate five to twenty minutes a day on being empowered. Start with 5 minutes and add a few more each day until you get to twenty. Try different ways. Use music one day and sit in silence on the alternate days.

ᚷ List your activities for one day and meditate upon the fact that you are more than your actions.

ᚷ Make a list of the skills you have that you use to feel empowered especially at times when you feel your motivation is waning.

POSITIVE PRAYERS

I LIVE IN EASE AND GRACE

I move and have my being in the Creator. As Spirit moves through me, its energy is my life force. Its momentum moves me to experience a closer connection to my Source, and I progress to a deeper awareness with every event. I flow with life in ease and grace.

The design, order, complexity, and beauty of the world around me provides abundant evidence for the existence of a powerful essence. This creation consists of the unlimited energy of God. I recognize that any troubles are ultimately due to the illusion of separation from the One. Any disorder is due to the subsequent separation from my Creator. My spiritual practice transcends this illusion and guides me on my path of enlightenment. I now allow my life to express freely; therefore, I embrace any challenge with open arms. I trust the process as divine activity directs my life.

I accept my path with thanksgiving and heartfelt gratitude, knowing I am always in the right place. This is truly letting go and letting God. And so it is.

FORGIVENESS SETS ME FREE

My God Essence is my perfect life. It is from this place that I live, move, and have my being. As the individualized expression of the divine, I rely on my creative intelligence, knowing it is divine activity.

I choose forgiveness today. Divine activity operates as me, providing the strength to forgive myself and others. Forgiveness is a cleansing process of releasing from my mind and heart those interpretations and perceptions of others, myself, and any experiences that bind me. In truth, I am a free spiritual being made in the image and of the qualities and essence of Spirit. I now activate spirituality in all my relationships by first acknowledging the perfection in everyone. The path to my greater happiness and well-being is unblocked by seeing the connection of all life. I remove any judgment around any experiences in which I felt harmed and enter into communion with God.

I am at peace, having liberated myself through forgiveness. I gratefully celebrate my freedom of mind, body, and heart. I let go. And so it is.

I PARTICIPATE IN RIGHT THINKING

Infinite intelligence is all there is. Its activity expresses in all areas of my life. I embrace infinite intelligence daily and watch my life unfold perfectly.

If I face a challenge, I engage the right thinking necessary to eliminate it. I separate myself from any challenge. Right now, I know I am more than my body. I am more than all the circumstances of my life. I am Intelligence, knowing the right decision to make. I have the power to handle any seeming challenge. I walk forward and release any ideas or situations that no longer benefit me. Knowing I am cause to all my experiences, I use the power of right thinking. This higher consciousness is happening now, unrestricted by any past experience. I have the right idea at the right time to make all right decisions.

I am grateful for divine intelligence present in every decision. My life is shining brightly. I live in the glow of infinite intelligence. And so it is.

I CHOOSE LOVE

Spirit's love is everywhere. Spirit as me, is love now. All I know is love, for I am one with God.

I declare that all I have going on in my life is happening as love: love of self, love of others, and love for all creatures in all forms. I choose to see love everywhere my eyes focus, including everyone I meet. I choose to hear love everywhere there is a sound. A world full of love surrounds me. My every decision is made from this foundation. When life feels challenging, I choose to accept it as another form of divine expression. My truth can only be love, as I am an expression of the magnificence of God. I give love at every opportunity. I am open to receive love, and I receive it daily.

With a grateful heart, I acknowledge love everywhere. I now release my word, knowing it is done in the mind of God. And so it is.

MY LIFE IS BEAUTIFULLY EXPRESSED

My God Essence is my perfect life. It is from this place that I live, move, and have my being. As the individualized expression of the divine. I rely on my creative intelligence, knowing it is Divine activity.

My consciousness brings my experiences to life. As a creative idea of mind, I have all the wisdom I require at the right moment to live a successful, fun-filled life. I know what to do, how to do it, and when to do it to function perfectly. I celebrate living in the flow. My still, small voice continually affirms my abundant life. As a part of the One Mind, I do not look to outward forms or circumstances for my relationships, health, or self-expression. God is the source of all life; therefore, I am free from depending on any one person, place, or thing for my good.

I know the divine continuously gives everything I desire in my life. I glide through my days wrapped in the arms of love. I trust in a Higher Power and have faith in myself. I choose life with heartfelt gratitude, and I dwell in it. And so it is.

INFINITE POWER IS MINE NOW

God is all there is. Everywhere I am God is. The infinite power of God is mine to use. I use it now and know that anything I choose to experience in my life awaits my recognition of it. I claim by right of divine inheritance, this power. It is available to me at all times.

Knowing my power, I look to express each day my highest and best. This shows up in a myriad of ways. However each is the authentic me; perfect, whole and complete. I show up in life and let my light shine.

Together with God, I move from good to greater good with ease and grace.

Appreciating who I am, a divine idea of God, I watch my life unfold in all its wonder.

Allowing these powerful words to return to the universe from where they came, I let go and let God.

You can reach the author at

cuyjetw@gmail.com

www.Facebook.com/Activating_the_Power_Within

www.Twitter@RevWaukena

www.ActivatingYourPower.blogspot.com